Eyes Fixed

MY TRUE LIFE STORY

T.C. STALLINGS

BroadStreet
PUBLISHING

BroadStreet Publishing® Group, LLC
Savage, Minnesota, USA
BroadStreetPublishing.com

Eyes Fixed: My True Life Story

978-1-4245-6047-9 (softcover)
978-1-4245-6048-6 (e-book)

Stock or custom editions of BroadStreet Publishing titles may be purchased in bulk for educational, business, ministry, fundraising, or sales promotional use. For information, please email orders@ broadstreetpublishing.com.

Typesetting by Kjell Garborg and design by Chris Garborg | garborgdesign.com

Printed in the United States of America
21 22 23 24 25   5 4 3 2 1

DEDICATION

This book is dedicated to everyone in my life who has ever played a role in my becoming the man that God designed me to be. None of us may know the exact number of people who influence our lives—but I am still and will always be forever grateful.

–T.C. STALLINGS

CONTENTS

FOREWORD
by Levette Stallings

There is an old metaphor that compares life or love to a roller coaster. That figure of speech couldn't be a more perfect description of my time with T.C., especially since we both love coasters. In fact, we love them so much that our honeymoon and a few anniversaries have consisted of trips to amusement parks. We love the joy and excitement that accompany the thrill as we stand in line for our favorite ride or that tight grip in our stomachs with a bite of fear as we are buckling up for the first time on that newest, fastest, record-breaking coaster, making us question if we made the right decision. These emotions can very easily correlate with the many ups and downs and twists and turns of our life together. June 9, 2021, will mark twenty years of marriage for us. As I think about that, I realize that we have been together for almost half of our lives, and I have had a front row seat to a great many of T.C.'s greatest accomplishments, his struggles, trials, and triumphs, many of which he will address in this book.

So often people just see your victories, but few know of the tears, hard work, or previous failures that brought you to them. There are things that my husband has endured and experienced that would have broken many. I remember when we first started dating and he would share stories of his childhood. As I listened to his plight, I tried but couldn't imagine walking in his shoes. My family wasn't rich by any means; however, my parents were happily married, owned their home, both had good jobs, and my brother and I never had to want for anything. It was such a stark difference from T.C.'s childhood experience. I couldn't help but admire his resilience. I think that's one of the things that drew me to him. I could see someone who, no matter what life threw at him, would keep going and wouldn't quit. He wouldn't let life's circumstances drag him down with them.

Being an athlete all my life, I have regarded actions more highly than words. Don't just talk a good game; back it up. You want to get better at your sport; are you practicing? You want to get stronger; are you lifting? You want to win; then what effort are you putting forth? So it was refreshing to be with someone who didn't just say that he was a Christian. I watched him put his faith into action. I could see that his strength came from his faith in Jesus. The things that he had experienced and endured through Christ shaped the man he was and pushed him to be better.

And T.C.'s road never seemed easy. There was always some hurdle he had to get over or some obstacle to overcome. Through his every hurt and disappointment, through every victory, through the joy and peace, even his times of extreme elation or the heartbreak of total defeat—I've marveled at his resolve to remain steadfast at seeking God's will and purpose through it all. He would say this prayer, which he still does today: *God, if this is from you, open the door. If not, please shut it.* It is this complete trust in God that makes the victories in his life that much sweeter because they are God's open door—*God's* yes. I've noticed that even when T.C. doesn't receive the outcome he has hoped for, initially there may be some disappointment, but it soon gives way to complete acceptance because he knows that when God says *no*, it's just as important as when he says *yes.*

We love to look back over our lives and see how God's puzzle pieces have fallen into place. Closed doors that didn't make sense at the time are completely overshadowed by God's open ones. Taking the time to see how God has been working throughout our lives makes trusting him that much easier. T.C.'s desire to pursue God's will and purpose has become the driving force of our family. Every aspect of our lives is embodied with this in mind. It is one of the main reasons why I would line up for this roller coaster ride over and over again. So I hope as you read T.C.'s story, you will be inspired; I pray that, just as I am, you will also be motivated and encouraged by his resolution that no matter life's burden, persecution, temptation, or even the promise of earthly rewards, nothing is worth compromising his faith and testimony and that you will see why T.C.'s eyes are so passionately fixed on Jesus.

Levette Stallings

PREFACE

Today, I can wholeheartedly say that I am extremely satisfied with my life. With stress, anxiety, depression, and all the many other challenges that come with being human, I feel very blessed to be able to say that nothing has prevented me from loving the life that God has called me to live. But loving life today has much to do with the events of my yesterdays and yesteryears. However, all these challenges that I am preparing to share with you have created a man who knows the importance of running *my own* race in life—and doing so to the best of my God-given ability—with my eyes focused solely on where God is leading me, *rather than where Satan wants to take me.*

I have been very hesitant over the years to tell my *full* story, to discuss all (or at least most) of my struggles and challenges. The main reason for my reservation is the fact that there is always someone in the world who will have had a much harder life, and I felt as though I'd been too fortunate to complain. But when I stopped questioning if my story was worth sharing (and I no longer compared my struggles to those of others), it became crystal clear to me why telling my story is important. Somebody needs to hear it, even if it were to be just one person. I reminded myself that—most likely—there is another "T.C." in this world who is facing (or will face) the same types of challenges that I have faced. This person (or these people) will experience the same kind of pain, disappointments, fears, or failures—all of which (in my case) were eventually counterbalanced with maturity, strengthening, courage, and success. The way that I handled things simply made me a better person in several areas. Stories like mine can be life changing for someone else. It would be a shame to keep it to myself. Maybe *you* are that "other T.C.," and my story is exactly what you need to hear today.

Before you dive into this book, I want you to know that I am not aiming to preach at you or teach you any particularly targeted lessons. This is not meant to be a devotional or a Bible study. This is just *me*. My life. Think of this as a friendly conversation; you and I sitting down to a cup of coffee or tea and simply having a real, candid chat. In fact, the remaining words written in this preface will be the closest things to me attempting to teach—and the only reason for that is because my story requires a bit of a setup. Context is everything. Knowing the heart behind this book will assist you in getting the most out of it—especially if you do not know anything about me at all. So just for a moment, I will go ahead and do the only small bit of "teaching" that I feel is necessary—which is simply me giving you the *why* of this book.

The story of my life is best summed up *as a relentless attack by Satan to distract me from my purpose, bump me off center, and cause me to ignore my God-given purpose in life*. Technically, for any Christ follower, this is the summation of your life too. The circumstances may be different, but the source and motivation are the same. The evil antagonist in your life is the same. Satan. The king of lies, evil, and temptation that can lead to sinful compromising within our relationship with Christ. A key word in all of this is *compromising*, which, in certain situations, is not always a bad thing. Compromising to reach a mutually positive result is not bad at all. For example, my wife and I compromise in our marriage whenever it is called for, which has led to a fulfilling, unselfish, wonderfully successful relationship. Positive compromising can apply to every area of life and will almost always yield a positive outcome. But, as with most things, an inherently good concept can always be perverted. Compromising is no different.

In a different context, compromising our walk with Christ in a sinful manner is one of the worst habits to develop. This lifestyle choice makes it so easy for Satan to have a negative influence in our lives and successfully distract us from the path we are designed to be on. God wants us to look "here" and "do this"; meanwhile, Satan tempts you to look "over there" and sinfully "do that" instead. Where we ultimately end up looking or going is heavily influenced by how much attention we pay to either promptings. How much time do we give Christ versus how much time do we spend entertaining Satan? And as we know, Satan doesn't need a ton of time in order to be destructive, deceiving, or misleading. Just ask Adam or Eve.

As Christians, we know Satan shouldn't get any of our attention. Ever. But I'm a realist, and I know that the struggle is real. I also know that we sometimes make it much worse of a struggle than it has to be. I've done that in my life. We know the choice is sinfully risky, but Satan is too persuasive. Sometimes we fall for his mess and allow him to lead us into thinking that "just a little bit" won't hurt. It is that right there—a small, dangerous compromise—that gets us into big trouble. Entertaining the voice of Satan and the temporary pleasures of sin can spiritually intoxicate us, and in many cases, it will heavily influence the decisions we make. And it makes sense why this is true.

We tend to follow our focus. Our gaze. If this focus is consistently on Jesus, sinning is much less likely to entice us and catch us up. On the other hand, eyes away from Christ on a regular basis (and sometimes, even just for a moment!) gives sin an open invitation to take the lead. And if Satan can get you to take your eyes off Christ and God's purposes for your life, then he has your spiritual temperature right where he wants it—*lukewarm*. Revelation 3:15–16 shows just how dangerous it is to find yourself in this situation:

> I know your works: you are neither cold
> nor hot. Would that you were either cold
> or hot! So, because you are lukewarm, and
> neither hot nor cold, I will spit you out of
> my mouth. (ESV)

A lukewarm life is one that can potentially make *us* happy while angering God. Why? Because lukewarm living cheapens our faith. We become willing to take sinful chances, risks, and concessions that—if we had been focused on Jesus—we would never have agreed to take. At least not so easily.

But that's just our sinful nature in our ear, powered by Satan, with the goal of disrupting our God-given flow, route, plan, and purpose—with a laser-focused intent of simply messing you up spiritually. I am talking about the literal act of trying to railroad the plan for your life that God himself took time to lovingly and purposely create. This is what has been happening to me my whole life, which brings me to the sole purpose of this book: to tell you how Satan has been attacking me from the beginning of my time on earth with the intention of compromising the plans that God intended for me.

Satan wanted me then (and now) to abort God's plan A for his tempting and sinful plan B. He has been relentless, which you will clearly see as I share all the details with you. But, from the very beginning, God has always been faithful. He has always fought for me. And although I have been spiritually hurt, tripped up, and even knocked down, I have never been knocked out. To this day, the main reason I can make this claim is because God has consistently found a way to keep me focused on the goal of becoming what he designed me to be. Even when I did not know how to keep my life centered on his will and my eyes focused on his purposes, his grace led the way so that I could eventually figure it out. And once I learned how to lock in on Christ and his purposes for my life, there was no turning back. But first—*I had to learn.* And I am about to share with you exactly how I did just that.

Many of these things will be hard to talk about. Some of these things may be a bit embarrassing for me. But I need to share them with you so that you can see how easily my life could have gone in a totally different direction from where I am now. Many people constantly heap praise on the person I am these days. They see how I live my life, and I am often told how much people admire me. But I will *never* take *any* credit for where I am today or the man I have become. All glory goes to God. Writing this book will help many people see exactly why I feel this way.

Satan nearly ran my life over on so many occasions. He was so slick and sneaky that, in most cases, I never saw him coming. I did not sense his presence as he stalked me throughout my life. Today, people love to acknowledge the level of spiritual strength and maturity that I have. But I tend to celebrate the fact that God sustained me for many years when I was extremely weak and spiritually immature. Long before I built even an ounce of spiritual strength, grew an inch of spiritual maturation, or knew anything about the importance of the Holy Spirit's power to fight sin—I was courted by Satan. Much too young (physically *and* spiritually) to recognize what was happening.

But *God*. His grace and his mercy never gave up on my ignorant, sinful soul. Unassumingly I entertained sin and its trapping pleasures, yet even then, my life and my purpose were both under God's protection. While Satan was planning and executing attacks, God was preparing and putting into action the many defenses and life-lessons that I would need. The best part of it all is the day I finally realized what was going on. I saw what God was doing. Then I became a willing participant in the plan that he had for my life. The road to this point of reckoning was long and bumpy at times. Painful. Scary. But as you are about to see—from the very first breath I ever was blessed to take—*it was purposeful.*

*"The most effective thing Satan can do
is to distract you from what God has called you to do."*

–T.C. STALLINGS

Chapter 1

DEFENSELESS

Cleveland, Ohio.

Few would argue this point: a baby being born is one of the most beautiful things anyone could ever witness on earth, in my opinion. But it can also become a tragedy when the people responsible for bringing the baby into the world are not ready for that responsibility. And that is how my story begins.

My birth mother and father were not prepared to have a child. I was not planned for. I was not prayed for. I was not expected. Initially, my mother was not even excited. She was not joyful. She was not celebrating. In fact, she was terrified, and she had good reason to be. My father (at this time in his life) was heavily affected by drugs and alcohol during my mother's pregnancy. He was in no condition to raise a son. Back then my mother did her fair share of drinking and partying as well. Because of these unhealthy lifestyles, my mother was fearful that if I were to be born, something could be terribly wrong with me. This was just one of the many things that gave my mother all kinds of fears about having me. Her financial stability was not the greatest, and her personal life was not where she wanted it to be just yet either. Both my mother and father had multiple children individually. They were not married. They were not happy with each other. They were barely involved in a meaningful relationship with each other. Then they found out that a huge responsibility was about to be added to the mix. Me.

As I said, my mother had other children before me—four by birth and one from adoption. So I had five siblings. But eventually, my mother shared with me that my birth should have constituted child number seven for my mom instead of six. Unfortunately, I don't have a sixth sibling because my mother aborted him. Or her. We will never know. As if this was not surprising enough, it was the next thing that she told me that truly shocked me. She nearly experienced a second abortion. She teared up when telling me how close she was to making that same decision again; only this time we were talking about *my* life. I didn't know how to process it. I can't explain the cryptic feeling I was having while listening to her describe what almost happened to me. Her circumstances easily could have been too much to consider any other alternatives. She was financially strapped. She was physically and mentally abused. She did not have the best social influences in her life at the time of her pregnancy with me. And she had already found the nerve to push through an abortion once before. She was very close to proceeding with another one— and there was nothing I could have done about it.

Today, my mother is probably my biggest and greatest cheerleader (other than my wife). She loves Jesus as much as she can these days. She loves going to church and loves to sing in the choir. She doesn't drink alcohol, she doesn't smoke, and she doesn't attend wild parties. With most decisions in her life, she knows that God must give her the okay to proceed. She prays for me. She loves me. She would give her life for mine right now, this second, if she had to. My mother is one of the best friends that I have. But in her early days, she used to be the exact opposite of everything I just said.

During the time of my mother's pregnancy with me, Satan had more of a grip on her life than Jesus did. Her life was "wild," in her own words. She made hasty and reckless decisions, she did what she wanted to do, and she had no respect for God's will. In fairness to my mother, she was not raised to be any different. In our talks about her childhood and early adulthood, she explained to me that it had been a long, hard life of trial and error that brought her to where she is today. Obviously, many of her lessons were painful ones. Hard ones. Losing me to the choice of abortion would have been yet another difficult lesson. I can't imagine having to confess to my child that I strongly considered aborting him. But she showed courage and wept her way through it.

We both struggled to discuss how my life nearly ended before it ever had a chance to start. It rocked my world to *sit and really think* about how close I came to losing the fight for my life. A one-sided fight, at that. I was defenseless, on the inside, at the mercy of people on the outside. I could not plead for my life. I could not tell her how much I loved her. She could not see me or look into my eyes. All I could do was wait in the womb while my life rested in the hands of two people whose lives were being torn apart by Satan. The circumstances were certainly not in my favor.

My parents never married. In fact, she left him during the pregnancy. He had his own set of problems that she felt did more harm than good to her life. My mother did not want him near her or me, and in her mind, any decision concerning my life was up to her, not my father—or anyone else. Of course, they constantly fought about this. The stress must have been crazy. I can easily see why it may have seemed easier to just get rid of me. My mother and I have such a great relationship today. These days, I talk to her just about every day on the phone. We laugh most of the time and act stupidly silly. She often tells me that the best part of her days are these goofy, silly phone calls because I always make her laugh.

To this day, my mother tells me that she doesn't really know exactly why she never went through with the abortion. She says that there were a lot of factors, including fear. With her first abortion, she was young and didn't really know what was happening. But with me, she was thirty years old, somewhat further along in her faith, and had a much more convicting conscience about what it would mean to abort the child that was growing inside of her. She literally had just enough of a relationship with the things of God to at least consider what he thought about what she was thinking of doing. Back then, she never directly credited her relationship with God for her decision not to abort me. But she contends that the little bit of Jesus that she had begun to experience at the time changed her heart. Talk about *a little bit going a long way.*

Neither one of us really cares about pinpointing exactly why she didn't do it, or how—while not the biggest Christian at the time—she still managed to eventually muster up enough faith in God to trust him with her pregnancy. And if you ask me, I'll tell you in a heartbeat why it didn't happen: because God said *no*.

He defended me. Before I ever took one breath on earth, my life—and the plan that God had for it—was already on the brink of being destroyed. And that's why I never forget to thank God for his sovereignty, grace, mercy, power, and love. I thank him for touching my mother's heart. Yes, humanly speaking, I was completely defenseless in the womb, but spiritually speaking, I was never without protection. And when I think about it now, even as I sit and write this chapter, I am experiencing the same kind of peace that I imagine I must have felt in my mother's womb. Think about that for a minute. On the outside, there was all kinds of turmoil in the lives of nearly everyone around me. Yet through it all, I just peacefully rested in the womb without a care in the world. No fear. No worries. All I knew how to do was control what I could control (which was mostly nothing at this stage) and let God finish what he started. And that is the most encouraging thing about all of this for me. His purposes prevailed. I was covered by God's plans, which are unstoppable, and in this case, he planned for me to live.

What a gift. What a tremendous blessing. And that is why, even now, I aim to live my adult life the same as I did while I lay defenseless in the womb. I try to remember to live a life that remains totally dependent on God. The only difference now is that I know him. I'm aware of his presence. I actually get a chance (every day) to play a role in God's plans by choosing to consistently be obedient to him. It is one thing to be a defenseless, unborn baby and having God fighting for you—but it's a whole different ballgame when (while living out your life) you know you have God's sovereignty, the leadership of Jesus, and the power of his Holy Spirit fighting for and through you.

When I came into the world on December 1, 1977, I wasn't held by both parents in the hospital room, celebrated by a happily married couple as they marveled at what they had accomplished together. My father was not even in the room. When he somehow found out when and where I was born, he showed up to sign the birth certificate—but even that was done out of spite. My middle name is comprised of his full name, obviously by his choosing. (For many years, I hated that my name came to be from such volatile beginnings.) My mother did not intervene in the birth certificate shenanigans, and instead, she chose her battles wisely. She simply fled the scene. Now that I was born, she was committed to fighting for me and getting me off to a good start.

I know my mother loved me from day one, but I still wonder to this day how December 1, 1977, really felt for her, due to all the stress. She tells me that she experienced great joy, even though she almost immediately went on the run and into hiding with me. My family unit was broken before it could ever get going. My mother began the task of trying to raise me (and five other kids) as best she could.

Obviously, I was not born into the greatest of circumstances, but I was born on purpose, with a purpose. Considering the alternative, simply having a chance at life was my first ever "big blessing," and it also marked the first huge hurdle of my life. It took my mother over thirty years to tell me this. I'm glad she did. She thought I'd be angry that she even considered having an abortion. But instead, I told her that I loved her even more because she rejected it. She trusted God to help her handle my birth. He gave her peace of mind so that she could think about allowing me to live. She had a choice: the easier life of continuing to raise the five kids she already had or making things tougher by bringing a sixth child into the mix.

She chose me. There is no way I could be mad about any part of that.

Chapter 2

BARE FEET

"Where is Toot? Where is that boy?"

Toot. That was my nickname growing up. Apparently, there was a popular song back in the 1980s in which the lyrics would say, "Don't mess with my toot-toot." Like most children who repeat anything they hear, I am told that I loved this song and would always sing along. Everyone thought it was cute the way I said "toot." And there you have it. "Toot" (or "Tooter" if you used my mom's version) was what everyone would call me. Sometimes when they called for me, I couldn't answer—because I was not in the house. Apparently, I would often slip out of our small apartment in the Cleveland projects and head to the local community center that often handed out free lunches. So whenever they noticed that I was missing, they knew where to find me. No shirt. No shoes. Not even a pair of socks. Just a little boy, maybe six or seven years old, sitting on the steps of the free lunch building wearing only a pair of shorts. Elbows resting on my knees, chin resting in my cupped hands, fingers tapping my face, waiting for a free lunch. Hungry, yet excited to get a sandwich, I just sat on those steps, staring at my two dusty little bare feet, waiting for the door to open.

This part of my story happened so early in my childhood that I don't remember it. So when my mother first told it to me (and she still does, all the time), I always have the same two thoughts. The first is that I think about how funny I must have looked—a half-naked little boy on the steps, first in line to get a free sandwich for lunch. But over time I begin to think about how blessed I was that I was never killed or kidnapped. Either of the two could very easily have happened in the inner-city housing projects of Cleveland where I grew up. But just like in the womb, the only thing I can attribute my safety to is God. Because drugs, crime, gangs, and other dangers were all around my family, the last word you can use to describe my childhood neighborhood is "safe." But it's obviously the first word that comes to mind when I think about how Jesus kept me. *Safe.*

My early childhood would be an indication of things to come in my life. I'd be raised rather loosely. This is not a shot at my mom or anyone else in my family. In fact, they were all raised the same way or close to it. It makes sense to me today why my upbringing was rather reckless because my mother's upbringing was the same. Nobody knew any better. While I was loved tremendously by my family and I was relatively pro-tected from most types of physical danger, I can't say that I was very well protected from spiritual dangers: Satan, sin, and temptation. Once again, this is no knock on my family, but none of them were very spiritual. They were not close to God. They were not true followers of Jesus or committed to obeying Scripture. They did not fear God. None of us really knew what any of that meant or looked like, so we all pretty much lived by our own sets of rules. Unfortunately, this truly made life hard for all of us. Harder than it had to be.

Being the youngest in my home, I did not have a whole lot of independent choices to make. Like any other baby of any family, I was always at the mercy of choices others made for me. I had to deal with the residual fallout from choices made by those taking care of me, both positive and negative. While I didn't learn a ton of spiritual or practical life lessons in my home, my mother did set one clear standard: *obey her*. That was easiest for me to adhere to, being the youngest.

I couldn't get into as many situations as my older siblings could, should they choose to. But, since all six of us fell under that command, I had the opportunity to learn from the mistakes of my siblings—allowing me to know what not to do in certain situations when I did become old enough to make my own decisions. There is a flip side though. The sin I witnessed did not always come across to me as wrong. Sometimes, it looked like it worked out and felt good. And since I didn't completely recognize sin for what it was, I looked at it as something I might try whenever I got a chance. Seeing the sin gave me a clear picture of what I could get myself into whenever I wanted to. I was always learning *something* from those in my home—whether they knew that I was or not.

I told you moments ago about me sneaking off from home for a free lunch. The reason I did this might be obvious—we did not have much. We were not poor in the truest sense of the word, but we were a low-income family, and we did struggle. The food stamps, the government cheese, and other handouts were essentials. We always kept a can of roach spray under the sink. We had the pliers on the TV to turn the knob, the metal hanger in place of the broken antenna. We had the little TV sitting on top of the big one that didn't work. I used to love fried bologna. Cheap foods. No worries, though. I was too young to understand the situation for what it was. If I saw a roach, I killed it and threw it away. It seemed normal.

I don't remember feeling one way or the other about what we had or didn't have during my youngest years. I think that does say a lot about the way I was treated. They treated me great. They loved me. They just didn't know how to love God yet or how to show me how to love him, so the type of examples that I had to learn from were very worldly. Loose. Wild by nature. Lots of drinking, smoking, profanity. Again, this was normal for us. So why change it? And as for me taking it all in, well, I was just a "baby"—a very young kid—so nobody really cared what they said or did around Little Toot. But as I got a little older and my awareness of my surroundings got clearer—I began to pick up on more things. With age and experience, there comes a time when you *do* start to make some of your own choices in life.

When I was about age eight, my family's culture began to make its mark on me. Behaviors. Lifestyles. Mannerisms. Habits. Standards. Choices. In all of these, some were good, and some were bad. This was one of the most important times in my life because these were the foundational years, where the concrete was being poured to form the foundation that I would build my life on. Satan wanted to influence the way my concrete was being poured, as he had already successfully done so with most of my family. Many of their hearts were already hardening towards the things of God. They, just as I was, were all attacked by Satan while at their weakest, pursued by sin when they were young, stalked by it and courted. Also, just as it was for me, I believe that God's grace was available to them too. But when they reached the decision-making age, they chose their own way of living, making it very hard to come to Christ. Because of this, Satan and sin were able to run rampant in the lives of my family, collectively and individually. It was only by God's grace that we were all able to survive our spiritually unhealthy family choices. But survival did not come easy or without consequences.

Little Toot, the youngest of them all, was downloading everything. Soaking it up like a sponge. Much of it I should never have seen, heard, or experienced. However, this is a great moment to highlight a crucial part of my life that my mother directly influenced. God used her to somewhat "balance me out." Yes, I was seeing a lot of sin in my family, but because my mother (by this time in her life) had become closer to Jesus, I, too, was placed on that path of getting to know him. To this day, I always say that I am glad that I was the youngest of six because, organically, I received my mom's best. As I was growing up, she was maturing with every year of her life. Yes, she partied hard for most of her life before I was born, but by the time I became a responsibility, she was thirty years old. She was ditching bad relationships for better ones. She was going to church more and more. Without these changes, I would have had 100 percent exposure to sin. All the time. But her newfound faith took her places that were making her a better person.

So half the time, I was hearing terrible language, but when she took me to church, I'd hear mostly wholesome talk. In my neighborhood and at home, sin was an easy temptation, but at church, vacation Bible school, church picnics, and youth events, sin was so much harder to find. Even today, as often as I can, I remind my mother how happy I am that she found Christ and let him begin to take over her life around the time that I was born. She wasn't perfect when I was a kid, but she was so much better than her previous years. This caused new rules to be implemented in the home. Bibles were lying around. Better role models visited our home. These things counterbalanced the sin that often hovered within its walls. I wish these things could have permeated my house completely, touching every-one in it. It would have made the battle much easier. But that certainly did not happen.

Chapter 3

IMPRESSIONS ON ME

When you are the youngest of six, all you can do is look up. I looked up to everyone around me in one way or another. I watched everything that they would do. It did not matter who it was or where they were from—if they came around me, I would study them. I'd listen to how they talked. How they acted. I'd watch all the mannerisms that were around me. I'd take mental notes. This natural habit made it easy for me to copy the behaviors of others. Maybe these were the early signs of the soon-to-be actor that God was designing me to be. I can't say for sure, but what I can say is that the things I saw growing up had a significant impact on my life, much of which was not so good. Of course, I had many good times too. But the bad times get the focus here because they are responsible for the near derailment of my life. The bad times were the vehicle that Satan used to deliver much pain and suffering. Fear. Division. Danger. Resentment. These things hit my family hard at times, and I had a front row seat to watch how my family handled them. These events would be my first impressions on how to deal with life. Initially my thoughts were that this is family, and they are doing a decent job of taking care of me. So in my young mind, there was no reason to doubt what they were showing me—especially if it didn't seem to be hurting anyone. Why not copy these behaviors too?

I didn't realize it then, but as I think back, I often witnessed Satan attacking the people that I looked up to the most, the people in my family. It's almost like Satan knew this would be a way to draw me in. He negatively influenced the lives of those that I would see, hear, and interact with the most, so their response to his enticements would serve as my example. My siblings loved me, and for the most part, they treated me great. But they had no clue on how to fight sin. Satan had his way. Growing up, they were never truly made aware of their spiritual deficiency. Some are still unaware. It's not necessarily all their fault.

Needless to say, in my younger days, I saw a lot of danger. I saw a lot of people hurt themselves and others. Worst of all, I saw sin play a regular trick on my family: success through sin. This is like a drug addiction. There are not many things in the world that are harder to stop doing than finding pleasure by sinful means. It's the simple gravity or magnetic attraction to pleasurable outcomes. Who cares how you get it—it just matters that you get it. Steal it. Manipulate your way into it. Lie for it. Cheat for it. Fight somebody for it. Whether it was friends in the neighborhood where I lived, family, friends of family, or even something crazy I saw on TV, I learned how to do all those sinful things. The consistency of what I was exposed to made it easier for me to learn it—and eventually, copy it.

I'll never forget the first time that I actually stole something. I was with my family at an amusement park. We rarely could afford to go places like this, so I loved it whenever it happened. I'm assuming most of you have been to an amusement park before, or at least you're familiar with them. So you know about all the enticing *smells* that are wafting past your nose all day. The popcorn. Caramel corn. Cotton candy. Pizza. Burgers and fries. The extremely oversized turkey drumstick. Funnel cake (Oh, man...funnel cake). Then there are the enticements for the eyes, with all the merchandise and souvenirs at the gift shops.

With all that being said, this was my dilemma: I didn't have any spending money. I usually never had extra money for stuff like that. We would always bring food from home to eat. Made sense. Whether you were wealthy or not, a lot of people did that. Nobody—no matter what your economic status was—wanted to pay $13.50 for a cheeseburger the size of a small cookie. But still, sometimes you want to buy things that you can only get at place like this (*funnel cake*). But I understood why my pockets were empty and why asking for spending money wasn't a good idea. These places usually cost $30 to $40 per person just to get into the park, plus the $10 just to park. (These days it's double and triple that.) For my mom to work hard enough even to get me there was already so cool. I needed to be content to just eat the food that we brought. The grilled pork ribs. The mac and cheese. The chips and juice. Good food too. (It wasn't funnel cake, but whatever. It was good.)

The food from home gave me a full belly, so that suppressed my appetite for all that expensive park food. Yes, even the funnel cake. But the gift shop was a different story. I didn't have a lot of toys at home. Seeing so many toys just hanging around in these huge gift shops did something to me. You all know where this is going, so I don't have to dramatize what happened. I stole a souvenir. But this is the weird thing about it: I don't even think it was about the souvenir. What I mean is, I don't think I really wanted the little toy that badly. And when I say little toy, I mean, *little* toy.

We were in a western themed part of the park, so they had these miniature keychain-size guns, with the park's name inscribed on them, displayed on an endcap. A very tiny, little thing. I took it and didn't even put it in my pocket. I just played with it in the store. Next thing I know, I'm pretty much out of the store, having played my way right out the exit. I absolutely realized right away that I still had the keychain. I could have returned it. But I also realized that they didn't know I had it. I could just leave. There were hundreds more of those keychains in there. So I pocketed the keychain and kept it. I didn't feel bad or anything. My theft didn't hurt anyone, as far as I knew. I had seen plenty of friends and family steal with no consequences. Now I was one of them too.

Oddly enough, while I felt no shame, I *did* know that I could *absolutely not* show my mother (or anybody else) what I had. She'd know I had stolen it. I just kept it in my pocket. Life goes on. My mother never knew about the keychain. She does now (sorry, Momma). She didn't hover over me enough in my personal world to even catch a glimpse of what I played with in my room. She'd probably agree that this was part of the problem, making it too easy to hide a sin or two. But she would also tell you that I was a very good kid, so she didn't see the need to constantly check on me. She counted on me to do the right things. And for the most part, I did. But that day at the park, I fell to the temptation to put into practice what I had seen others do so many times before in my life. I'd learn as I got older to become less tolerant of sin and temptation. But most of my younger years did not come with a ton of examples of spiritual convictions.

The Bright Side

With all the negativity I speak of, I can't just ignore the few *good* examples and role models that I saw. Of all my siblings, one did graduate high school. My middle sister. I'll never forget seeing her walk across the stage in her cap and gown. My mother was so proud. I wanted to do that someday too. Finish school and make Momma smile. My eldest brother was a great boxer. He won a few junior tournaments and had boxing trophies all over the house. My mother loved that. He was (and still is) an amazing mechanic. Can fix anything on a car. My other brother (the middle brother) was very popular in school. He kept up with the styles and knew how to keep a girlfriend. I'm blushing right now because I used to try to be just as smooth as he was. He was the one I spent most of my childhood growing up with. (I also used to sneak and wear his clothes since they were better than mine!) My other sisters were responsible for a lot of the fun because they started families at early ages. That gave me plenty of nieces and nephews. When my sisters moved out on their own, they would often welcome me to their homes to spend the night and hang with my nieces and nephews. Usually, they had boyfriends that were always nice to me and spent time with me playing video games or giving me a few dollars to run to the corner store, allowing me to "keep the change."

And of course, there was my momma. My mother hardly *ever* missed a Sunday at church, and if she went—*we* went. She sang in the choir and was on the path to becoming solid in Christ. She literally was the only trace of spirituality in our home (until my stepfather entered the picture during my middle school years). For all this, I thank God. My life wasn't *all bad*. There was a bright side to look on, a side that many stories do not have. But unfortunately, the good was often suppressed by the bad—seemingly all the time.

Too Much Room

We gave Satan too much space in our family. Too much room in too many hearts. Good times got drowned out by bad ones. Sin was suffocating us, so the goodness couldn't truly breath, stay alive, and stick around. And that's the point. This is the reason I'm highlighting the sin in my family so much. The good wasn't the problem; *the bad was*. And the bad threatened the ability to learn from anything good because the bad so often dominated the good. And those closest to me, always around me, never understood that they were constantly imprinting on my life. They were constantly contributing to the process of shaping me. Satan would throw in a heavy dose of chaos that would almost always overpower anything that felt right. This was my family.

At age eight or nine, I just began to accept that this was how it was supposed to be. This is what the Stallings do. Follow their lead. Trust what I see. Get used to it. Grow comfortable with it. Become numb to it and don't expect much more. These became my own personal prevailing thoughts. So I did just that until what I was looking at began to frighten me. There was so much violence. People were getting shot. I witnessed domestic abuse. Gang fights. Imprisonment. Drugs. Drive-by shootings. Police raids. These things began to become all too common in my young life, and it scared me.

It wasn't all the time. It wasn't every day. Again—I can't negate all of those good, safe, secure days, like the weekends at the church. School was fun most of the time. So were the family gatherings at my granny's house and playing with my friends either at their houses or mine. These were the good times that I am grateful for. But I'm telling you—I know Satan must have hated to see us happy as a family because it felt like he never let our joy last, stick, or stay. It was always crazy how we could be happy one day then easily find ourselves messed up the next. In one way or another, sin would find a way to wreak havoc. Someone I loved would get shot. Go to prison. Get in a fist fight. Start a terrible argument. Something would manage to steal the joy away. I hated to see this.

You might say, "T.C., I loved hearing about your good times! Please tell us about more those!" Well I'd certainly love to focus on them as well. But the truth is, it wasn't the good times that shaped me and had the greatest impact on the man

I am today. It was, in fact, the struggles. I hated the struggles, but now, I can't deny how much I've grown as a result. God redeemed and repurposed all these negative experiences for my good. The up-close view that I had of sin tearing up my family gave birth to some ambitious personal goals (starting at an unusually young age). Many times, it was these negative imprints and impressions that made me question myself this way: *Do you want this to be you, T.C.? Do you want to have a life that resembles the pain and dysfunction that you see?*

So I talk about my struggles more than my success because I saw more struggles than successes—and learned more lessons from them (at least this was the case in my early childhood). One such struggle—a family fight—taught me the lesson of a lifetime. It was terrible, and once again a day that I will never forget because it changed everything for me. The only good thing about this fight, ironically, was that we were not fighting each other.

God Was Fighting Too

My family literally had a brawl in the streets with another family. Let me give you a bit of context first. One thing that will always be true about my family is this: if they think there is a good enough reason to come together—for a positive or negative goal—they will quickly unite. Another thing that my family would never hesitate to do is to defend one of our own. If someone made the decision to put their hands on one of my family members, then that person just asked to be confronted by nearly everyone in my family. Fights and arguments were common in my neighborhood and occasionally in my home. No big deal. But I had never seen one full family fighting another full family in the middle of the street. Yet this is exactly what happened.

Some guy who lived on my sister's street made the mistake of hitting her. She called everyone in the family, lighting a match that fired up every one of us. This wasn't hard to do to us back in the day. From all over the city, from their various homes, my family jumped into their cars and headed to my sister's street. I was only about nine or so. I had *no idea* what I was about to see. In fact, consider that the following is the PG-13 version of what I saw. I don't even want to fully describe it. It depresses me to revisit it. It was that bad. Especially for my young eyes and ears.

We pulled up to my sister's house, and she was still arguing with this guy and a few members of his family. She was still upset that she had been struck, and we then realized that she had been struck by more than one person. This guy's girlfriend was in on the act too. My sister's yelling revealed these details. And that did it. My family confronted theirs, and fists began to fly. There was fighting and bloodshed going on all around me. People were getting seriously hurt. I was the only child from either family there, standing in the street unattended, with fighting all around me. Just about every member of my family was matched up against a member of the other family.

I was standing there all alone, scared and not sure what to do. As this fight went on, I noticed one of my family members appearing to be in a bit of trouble. I felt as though something needed to be done; I just didn't know what, exactly. But this is where those negative childhood experiences that had made such an impression on me kicked in. This is where I did what I had always done: copy what I see. They were in a fight, so I needed to fight too. I needed to help them. To *do* *something*. I looked to my right, and I saw a white curtain rod lying on the curb. I picked it up and went charging at this person who was getting the better of someone from my family. I remember yelling as I was running, "Get off my family!"

I headed straight for this person's head with the intent of knocking them out with this curtain rod. In my mind I was telling myself to swing as hard and as fast as I could. When I got close enough to hit this person, suddenly I was grabbed up. It was my stepfather. Initially, I didn't know who grabbed me, and I didn't like it. I began to squirm wildly, attempting to get loose. I really wanted to get *my* hit in. I wanted to help. I wanted to join the fight. That's what families do. But my stepfather said no. I remember him yelling at me saying, "No, don't you hit them! This is not what you do—stop—get over here so that you don't get hurt! Put that down right now and stand here with me."

Man, I was so upset. Then quickly I got sad. Then extremely confused. Then angry.

I just began crying. I remember being frustrated because I thought I was doing the right thing. But once I snapped out of my little, young rage and put the curtain rod down, I looked back out at all the people getting hurt and beat up and slammed to the ground. It just made me cry more. I went from wanting to help to hating what I was seeing. I hated the violence. The blood. The yelling. The fighting. The danger. All of it.

And that's the *big* positive that I could pull from this fight. It's the fact that I never got a chance to enjoy fighting.

Had I successfully struck the person that I was trying to hit, followed up by a pat on the back by my stepfather for my efforts (instead of a God-led harsh rebuke), there is no telling what my perspective on violence might be today. Violence, vengeance, and fighting could easily have become a way of life for me from that point on (as it did for so many of the people that I grew up around). Quarreling and knocking people out could have become my preferred method of solving my problems. But instead that moment led to a complete 180 in thought, desire, perception, and emotion.

Not only that, but I also starting to set goals for myself that were directly related to that family fight experience. I remember telling myself that I never wanted to be in a situation like this again. I never wanted to see my family fight. I never wanted to have to hurt someone. I didn't want to be in a family that fights with other families. So I promised myself that when I got my own wife and kids, we would never let something like this happen. I promised! I was so young when I began to make these goals for myself. And that's just it. That's the beauty that I can see in all of this. I was at the decision-making age, where the foundation of my life was being shaped. Satan tried to use the people that I love the most, taking advantage of the trust I had in them, to teach me violence. Bloodshed. Dysfunction. But God said *no*. He used my stepdad in a mighty way. While I didn't get into the fight, God certainly did. He was fighting for me because I was too young to fight for myself.

Chain Breaker

My family consisted of plenty of talented people. But the story always seemed to be the same: sin would get in the way before any of them could use their gifts in a positive way. It had happened to everyone I knew, and I seemed to be next in line. But I didn't want that. I wasn't okay with that possibility. I started to want something different. I wasn't sure exactly how to go about it though. Nobody ever sat me down to discuss goals. If not for the fight, I'm not sure that I would have chosen to set them for myself. But what motivated me was the real possibility of never escaping the stress of living a "rough" life. I didn't want it for myself or my family—especially my mother.

It was around this time that I started to recognize some of my gifts. Acting, athletics, and communication. I started to get involved in every church or school play whenever I could. My first big performance at a school function was re-enacting the Michael Jackson "Billy Jean" video for a school talent show. I won! All my brothers and sisters were there. My mother designed my performance outfit. She got me a black suit and white collared shirt and a black derby hat. I was on the Usher Board at church, so she used one of my white usher gloves and sewed some sparkly material on it from one of her dresses. She did the same thing with my white socks. I was glittering at the ankles in my highwater black slacks, and my right hand was sparkling too. I went out there on stage with my classmates as my background dancers and did my thing. When the crowd cheered at the end, and my family cheered even louder, I knew that performing in some way would be

EYES FIXED

something I would grow to love. I wasn't quite sure about the type of performing that I wanted to pursue, but I just knew I loved making people feel something. Inspiring people. Making others happy, especially my mother. Looking out there, seeing her grinning ear to ear—that made my day. The great reception from the talent show led to me taking any (and all) opportunities to perform.

I followed my mother's lead and began singing in the church choir. Solos, youth concerts, you name it—I did it. Easter plays, skits, whatever put me in front of people. I'd be playing in my room, and Momma would have guests over, then all of a sudden, I would hear my name called, followed by, "Come on down here and do the Michael Jackson!" And I'd knock it out for her and her friends. Gladly.

My mother was always so proud of me growing up. Not much changed when I became an adult. She still never hesitates to tell me whenever I make her proud. In her words, she'd say, "Boy, I'm so proud of you that my chest sticks out like Dolly Parton's." Mind you, I have been hearing this since I was five years old. It took several years before I had any clue what she meant by this. I didn't even know who Dolly Parton was, but once I got older and realized who she was, I realized that my mother must be *really* proud.

Chapter 4

WHAT COULD'VE BEEN

I often find myself thanking God for his grace in my life. I get overjoyed when I think about all the close calls in my early childhood. Before I learned how to passionately strive to obey God, I would struggle with temptation—in several areas—daily. And I'm not talking about a little keychain thievery. As you get older, the temptations get more sophisticated. Earlier I talked about how I would always see so much sin around me and how I didn't have the best examples. So it would be easy to simply blame my choices on those responsible for raising me, but I can't completely do that. Some of my choices were simply due to my own spiritual immaturity or selfish desires.

I told you that I attended church nearly every Sunday. Do you think all those Sundays were filled with Bible lessons, sermons about good choices versus bad choice, and fearing God? Sure, they were. You think my mother didn't have me fearing repercussion if I disobeyed her? Sure, she did. But I hadn't yet learned how to apply these biblical lessons to my life in a meaningful, purposeful way that would stick, and, when it came to my mother's discipline, I didn't have a ton of accountability and oversight from her. She'd usually have to "catch me in the act" or stumble upon a mistake I was making, and then she'd correct it. So as a result, I learned most of life's lessons the hard way—on my own—by falling to temptation and experiencing the consequences. While these lessons proved to be beneficial, that doesn't mean that learning the hard way is preferred.

When I say I learned hard, I truly mean it. *Hard.* In many cases, I could have gotten myself killed. Carried off to prison. I could have become a teenage father. A drug dealer. A gang member. Yes, I had opportunities to easily travel down these roads, and I tested the waters in all of them. I basically "put a toe into the shallow end." I never got too deep with my bad choices—but I *could* have. All the conditions were right for this to be the case. My run-ins with these temptations could easily have changed my entire life, and, if not for God's grace, they most certainly would have. They would have made becoming the man I am today much harder, maybe even unlikely.

It creates a mixed bag of feelings when I really consider the pitfalls that the grace of God allowed me to avoid. In this bag I have regrets because of the pain of the lesson, and in that same bag is the satisfaction of who I have become as a direct result of being pushed through this same pain. But my greatest emotion out of this bag of emotions is gratitude to the Lord. Without God protecting me and his purpose for my life, I can only imagine what could've have happened. As I said, in some cases, I'm talking about life and death.

Near Death

When I was in junior high, I was nearly killed in my own home. How did I get myself in that kind of predicament? Unintentionally. But sin was at the root of it. A love for inappropriate movies, TV shows, and music filled my brain with bad ideas. Everyone my age was listening to and watching the same sinful content. We loved it. Profanity, sex, drugs, violence—this kind of entertainment was the norm, and the residual effect of regularly consuming this stuff led to the eventual copying of the improper behaviors, mannerisms, and language. I will not blame the entertainment industry and culture as the sole reason for my issues because, as always, nobody was twisting my arm to listen or watch. The artists behind the music and the shows did not force their way into my stereo or TV. But it is fair to say that the existence of it and my ability to experience it certainly played a role. It was highly influential. And at one point, the mimicking of these actions— things that just seemed like innocent fun that I'd picked up from a popular movie—almost cost me my life.

It starts with my big brother's solid black 9mm air pistol. I loved it. It looked exactly like a real handgun. My mother would never buy me a BB gun like that at my age. But nothing was wrong with my brother having one at all. He was four years older than I was. He had his own money and bought what he wanted. So I used to sneak and play with that BB gun without permission all the time. I was just trying to be cool like the fellas in the films we would watch. It was cool to be "gangsta" back then (for some, it still is today). It was normal though. Gangs and street activity were regular, daily things for me. I wasn't directly involved, but I didn't have to be in order to experience it. See it. Feel it. It was everywhere. Outside my door, across the hall, in my neighborhood, at my school. And in the movies or music that my friends and I would often entertain ourselves with.

I had a best friend in the neighborhood that I did everything with. We wanted to be gangsta rappers ourselves and even tried to start a group. That's a story for another day, but needless to say, it didn't work out. But it was still fun to act gangsta. Dress like them. Talk like them. One of our favorite terms from the hood movies was "break yourself," meaning, "I'm taking something from you, and you better not try and stop me." Well my friend and I were not into robbing people. We just liked to say, "Break yourself," yelling it as loud as we possibly could—right up in your face. Better yet, to catch you off guard with it and scare you from behind with a loud one. For fun, one of our favorite things to do was jump out unexpectedly from hiding somewhere and scare one another half to death. We could be anywhere, and one of us would (unbeknownst to the other) slip away and hide. Then the other person would end up searching, knowing that at some point, somebody was going to jump from behind a wall or something and say, *"Break yourself!"* We would yell it at the top of our lungs while pointing our hands at the other person's face in a gun-like gesture. We loved playing this game. It was just something we picked up from one of our favorite movies starring one of our favorite rappers.

One day, my friend got me good. He called me over to his house. He left the door open so that I could enter his home by myself—something that he would always do, so I thought nothing of it. Then he popped out of nowhere, catching me off guard while yelling, *"Break yourself, fool!"* Scared the daylights out of me. He got me good. And of course, I was already plotting my revenge.

A few days later, we had a no-school day. I decided to ask my friend to come over early to hang out at my house and play video games. This was my chance to pay him back for scaring me so badly the other day. Both of my parents were at work, and I was home alone. Perfect. Because my plan was *not* to surprise my friend by jumping from around a corner. Instead, I was going to let him knock, tell him to come in, and then when he opened the door, he'd be face-to-face with what he would perceive as a real 9mm handgun. We'd always pretend our hands were pistols, but we had never used any kind of gun. Not even a water gun. So I knew that not only would the BB gun terrify him, but he might pee his pants thinking the gun was actually real! Where we lived, having guns in the house was the norm, so it wasn't out of the realm of possibility that I could've gotten hold of a real one from somewhere. I knew I'd trick him!

I quickly went to get my brother's BB gun. One problem—I could not find it! Did he take it with him? I didn't know. I looked everywhere for it. Did he hide it from me? I tore our room up looking for this thing. Pretty soon I just gave up. But I still wanted to do something to get my friend back. Next thing I know, I hear a knock at the door. I was out of time.

Since I couldn't find the gun, I just gave up on scaring him because my attempt would now just be lame. But of course, I still planned to get him at some point. The knocks continued, so I went to let him in. I opened the door, and it was *not* my best friend. It was five policemen, all with their guns drawn. Extremely bright flashlights blinded me, and there was lots of *intense* yelling: "Back up! Back up! Sit in that chair! *Now! Do it right now!* Sit down, *now!*"

They yelled so fast, so loud, and so intensely, that I froze. My heart thumped against my chest. I was stuck. Finally, I snapped out of it and put my hands up. Then I started backing up until I fell onto the seat of our recliner. The police rushed in and searched our entire home. I had no idea what they were looking for or why they were there. This whole ordeal may have taken ten minutes, but it felt like forever. Then, just as fast as they came in, they left. They didn't say anything else to me; they just left. I didn't go anywhere. I was frozen solid. Terrified.

A lot of time passed, and I still had not moved. It was so quiet in my house now, just the sound of the television playing low. And the still thumping sound of my heart kept going and going. I thought about moving, maybe going to the phone and calling somebody. But I really thought something bad would happen if I got up. What if they were watching from outside? What if they decided to come back and I was running around? I didn't know what to think. Then another thought hit me: *What if I had found my brother's BB gun?* I would have opened the door thinking my friend was on the other side. I planned to open the door and yell, "Break yourself"—and I'm pretty sure they would have killed me. The thought of that possibility scared me all over again. I stayed put. Nothing was going to get me out of that chair.

For the next few hours, I sat in the recliner, too shook to do anything else but cry. I didn't move a muscle until finally my mother got home from work. She immediately knew something was wrong. And when I described to her what had happened, she was furious. I had seen my mother upset before but not like this. She called the police department and gave them more than a piece of her mind. Meanwhile, I was changing my mind about how cool it is to copy the violence that I'd seen in movies. Doing so nearly cost me my life. Thank God for his grace. *Thank God I never found that gun.*

Depression?

This next little piece of information is something that I have rarely talked about publicly because I have always tried to forget it. It was a way of thinking that used to literally steal my joy all the time. After this incident, all the way up to my sophomore year of college, I struggled with a fear of death. It was an off and on type of feeling that would just drop on me, seemingly out of nowhere.

During my junior high school years, our class would some-times go to the planetarium. The teachers would start talking about how the earth was formed, and the "Big Bang Theory," and the many galaxies, and the black holes. Of course, I'd pay none of this any mind because at church I had learned that God created everything. But while the planetarium slideshow played on, I started to ask myself questions that my finite little human mind could not answer. While I was convinced that God created everything, I wondered who created him? How could he just pop into existence?

Then I started to think about how I seemingly popped into existence. I wondered how God made me and why? Then I would think about how, one day, I had to die. That scared me. Sure, I had learned about heaven, but I didn't understand it. And even with that, I wondered how eternity worked. Do we just live on for a trillion years? Then what?

It just didn't make sense to my young mind, and I would put my head down as if I were taking a nap and just cry. The anxiety was just too heavy. They inability to wrap my head around eternity with Christ was frustrating. These episodes and the fear of it all always ended in anxiety attacks. The thought of death simply scared me. The inevitability of it ter-rified me even more. The mystery of it angered me. I'd cry about it in my bedroom at night, too, the same way I did at the planetarium. I never told anyone about this.

As I got older, these anxiety attacks never stopped, but they did become less frequent. The reason (I assume) is because staying busy usually helped me *not* to think about death. Exciting and fun things such as parties, football, going to the movies, and other social events always served as a great distraction. It got to the point that I depended on these things anytime I even thought my mind was "going there."

But after a while, it was as though these thoughts just changed their schedule and began to come to my mind *after* the fun was over. Any fun-filled high that I was on from a good film, a rollercoaster, and sometimes even a good game would come crashing down. The prevailing thought would be, *What does it matter how fun this was? We all have to die someday. Then what?* It almost felt like death was a bully that kept reminding me how much tougher than me it was and how I would never be able to beat it. If there was ever a time in my life that I could say I was on the brink of giving up, this would be it. Personally, from what I've come to know about depression, I don't think I ever fully got to that point. But it just amazes me how something so heavy could weigh on a mind so young.

Of course, even now, I still can't say that I can fully wrap my head around eternity. Nobody can. But I thank God for what he has done in my mind these days, as I've certainly matured in Christ over the years and have long gotten past those old feelings of anxiety. In fact, there is a sense of peace that allows me to enjoy life every day, and I let the promise of eternity comfort me, rather than letting the inevitability of death cause me fear. The very mysteries about the beginning and the end, and the fact that my finite mind struggles to process the infinite, are now the things that make me say, "There must be a God." I don't have enough faith to believe the opposite. What crippled my mind is now the fuel that pushes me even closer to God.

But back when I was young, I didn't really know how to think of death and eternity this way. My young mind truly had a lot to process. Maybe too much.

Almost Joined

Most of my childhood, I lived around gangs and gang violence. Fights, shootouts, and drive-bys were normal. Graffiti everywhere, people getting arrested, wild parties with drugs and alcohol—these were things I witnessed regularly while I was growing up. Many of the men in my family ran with gangs. My brothers were in gangs. I was used to it. I saw it either in movies or in my own back yard. I watched gang initiations all the time. Pretty much, all of my friends had big brothers who were in the same gang, and we little brothers hung together just as much as the gang brothers did. It didn't take long before the hood decided to form a junior gang consisting of all the little brothers. Initially, I wanted nothing to do with it. But I was in the minority, and the temptation to join rather than be left out won me over. The older brothers took a few days to initiate us. By the end of the week, I was in the junior gang.

Only a few days later, the older brothers got into a fight with a rival gang at school. The fight traveled outside of school. Later that night, the rival gang drove through our neighborhood and opened fire as the car passed by. We all ran into our houses. Honestly, I wasn't all that worried because the gang was shooting at the older boys farther down the street, not me and my friends. But what did scare me was the thought of getting shot. The thought of getting caught in a crossfire. Getting shot by mistake was bad enough, but it was a whole different thing to be targeted because you are affiliated with a gang. I took off the gang colors and refused to participate. Sadly, many of my friends kept going. Today, some of those very friends are either dead or in prison—including one of my best friends from childhood. That truly could've been me. But thank God, my little "gang membership" experience only lasted a couple days. I never got the chance to embrace that kind of lifestyle.

More "Almosts"

There were a few other key "almosts" and "could-have-beens" in my life. This next one was fueled by the fact that I grew up as a "have not" for most of my childhood, and when you spend so much time around the haves, you can sometimes become envious. Stealing my brother's much better clothes wasn't worth the constant arguing that resulted from it. Borrowing my friend's nice hats or shirts got old real quick. Now I do not want to paint the picture that I didn't have *anything* nice to wear. Of course, I had a few things. My mother did her very best to get me a few pairs of nice jeans, a few shirts, and at least one pair of nice shoes for school. My basic needs were met. I just had to take care of what I had. But for the most part, money was a bit of a struggle. In my neighborhood, if you struggled, then selling drugs was the easiest way to fix that. This was a route that many in my neighborhood chose to take.

Drug dealers were all around me. I knew many of them personally. One of them nearly changed my life for the worse by giving me a very intriguing offer. Being familiar with my money struggle, he offered to help change that situation. It was simple; all I had to do was be a runner for him. Being *a runner* simply meant that he would give me small amounts of drugs, and I would take them to his customers for him. He would pay me a small amount of money for doing it. Normally,

I would be scared to do something like this, but the person who coached me to do this was somebody that I trusted, someone that I looked up to. He had the cars and the money from doing the exact same thing that he was asking me to do. He told me—point blank—that this little job would end my money struggles. The temptation was very strong, so I agreed to do it that same night. He gave me the drugs, and I ran to go drop them off.

When I got to the house, I was met by a strange look-ing woman with money in her hand. She wanted the drugs first. She took them from me and immediately put them in her mouth. She was testing them. But the way that she was testing them was dramatic and scary. She looked like a zom-bie, and as she made the zombie-like noises, her eyes rolled to the back of her head. Then other people started to come. I became extremely uncomfortable and afraid. I just left. I didn't even get the money. I either forgot or just didn't care; I can't remember. I just wanted to get as far away from that place as possible. I remember telling the person who had me selling for him that being a runner was not for me. So on the same night that my little drug dealer career began, it also ended. *This was another moment when Satan almost got me.*

There would be other close calls like this, and just like the drug dealing fiasco, they all could have changed my life for the worse. One of the most memorable situations put me in a place where I never thought that I would be—a jail cell. All my life I grew up watching people go in and out of jail. I had to visit several family members there, leading me to promise my mother that I would never end up in prison. She would always tell me that she was tired of going to see her sons in prison, and it would make her happy if she never had to come and see me there. This became a new reason to stay out of trouble. So although there were always plenty of sinful opportunities to have fun or make money, I would tend to avoid them. I still had other sinful bad habits, though, such as using profanity, watching bad movies, and listening to explicit music.

At this stage of the game, I wasn't trying to avoid trouble with the aim of pleasing God in mind. I didn't even think God cared about what I did. I just figured belief in him was enough to keep me right with him. Staying out of trouble was more about my mother. I was just trying to please *her.* But a lapse of judgment on a warm summer day put that plan in jeopardy.

It was around the Fourth of July, so everybody had been buying firecrackers and fireworks. Among the most popular kinds were "smoke bombs." These little bitty round balls would let out huge plumes of smoke after you lit the wick. My friends and I had a ton of these. One of my friends got the crazy idea to go house to house and drop smoke bombs through people's mail slots. In the apartment complex where I lived, all the apartment doors were inside narrow, enclosed hallways, and a small mail slot was on each door. The mailman could come and easily push the mail through the slots, and it would fall right onto the floor inside the home. We thought it would be funny to drop smoke bombs through these mail slots and watch as the smelly, pungent smoke rose. This was meant to be a harmless prank. At worst, people would be mad at the smoke and the smell, but we knew that the smoke would eventually dissipate, and the smell would go away.

Making it a point to avoid our friends' homes, we only went to the apartments where we didn't know the people who lived there. We would take turns dropping smoke bombs through the mail slots, run and hide, and then watch for their reactions. But what we forgot about was the little flame of fire that would ignite from the smoke ball's hole for about five to ten good seconds immediately after all the smoke was released from the ball. This hadn't been a problem for the people that did not have carpeted floors, so it was all fun and games until one of the homes just so happened to have a carpeted floor. And unfortunately for me—this bomb was dropped *on my turn.*

A small part of the carpet in this apartment caught fire from the flame of the smoke bomb, but my friends and I didn't know this had happened. We had dropped the bomb in the house, saw the smoke rise, then ran off laughing to the next apartment. It would be hours later that I would discover that a little fire had started at one of the apartments. Once we had finished smoke bombing apartments that afternoon, I went home to get something to eat. When I came back outside to reconnect with my friends, I could see off in the distance that the police were at one of the apartments that we had bombed.

Once I saw the police car, I got scared and ran back home. I completely changed clothes and then went back outside. In an effort to create the illusion that I had nothing to do with it, I actually went over to the apartment where the police were and just stood there with all the other people who were wondering what was going on. I, too, was asking what was going on, even though I already knew. But I simply thought the people who lived in the apartment were just mad about the smoke. So when I heard that the carpet had caught on fire, I felt both afraid and terribly remorseful. I remember thinking to myself, *Why did it have to be the house that I bombed?* I was fortunate that the fire was put out quickly and did not have a chance to spread; it never grew more than half a foot. I thought about what could have been, and I literally wanted to throw up. I had avoided a disaster, yet I think God still wanted me to learn a big lesson from this reckless choice. What he allowed to happen next played a huge role in the direction of my young life.

Scared Straight

As I stood along with the crowd that was watching the smoke bomb investigation, something interesting was happening. I watched the woman standing outside of her apartment talking to the police, and the longer I stood there just a few feet away from her, the more I realized that there was a good chance I would not be caught. And while I felt terrible about what I had done, I felt better knowing that it appeared I would probably get away with it. I didn't want anyone to know that I was responsible for doing such a terrible thing. For the moment, changing my clothes and strolling back up to the scene of the incident appeared to have saved me.

Had I been right about this assumption of having "dodged a bullet," it wouldn't have been a good thing. Because there's always the chance that I would remember how to deceive people and protect myself if ever caught in a similar situation. But I would find out moments later that I had not, in fact, gotten away with anything. This became clear when a second policeman walked out of the apartments, and my friends were with him. My heart dropped into my stomach when they pointed me out. But I understood. I wasn't even mad.

I figured this was about to be the moment where the police were going to wag their fingers at us and tell us not to do something like this again. But that is not what happened. At least not to *me*. The smoke filling the home was bad enough, but the fire was a whole different story. Being that I was the unlucky one who tossed the smoke bomb into the home that started the fire, my lesson turned out to be much harsher. When the policeman started to approach me, my heart began to *thump*. Even though I only expected a verbal reprimand, the sight of him approaching me did not feel good. And that feeling became much worse when he said, "I need you to turn around and put your hands behind your back." I could not believe it. I had promised my mother that I would never go to jail. But the clicking of the handcuffs as the officer adjusted them around my wrists reminded me that I had broken my promise. They read me my rights. I still couldn't believe it. I'd seen this happen to plenty of other people but never thought it would happen to me. They put me in the car and drove me out of my neighborhood. They took me to jail.

When I got to the jail, they put me through the whole process. Fingerprinted me. Removed my shoelaces. Took my belt. Then they led me through a few large doors and locked me in a small cell. They let me sit there for quite a while. Later, they asked me to make a call and notify my legal guardian. Both my parents were at work, so I called a friend of the family and informed her of my embarrassing situation. After that, they took me back to the cell with nothing to do but think. And of course, all I could think about was letting my mother down. I thought about how half the block just watched me get carried off to jail. I was immediately humbled. I never thought I'd be sitting in a jail cell. What was really just a few hours felt like an eternity. The weight of regret set in and the *Man, I wish I would have never* quotes kept running through my mind.

Probably the thought that made the greatest impression in my head that day was the fact that my goals for life could not be achieved in an eight-foot jail cell. Getting out of my dangerous neighborhood was not supposed to mean trading it for prison. Finally, my resolve kicked in. Now, all of the *Man, I'm never coming back here* thoughts began to take over my mind. I decided that this would be the first, last, and only time that I'd enter a jail as a troublemaker. And as it turns out, this is exactly what the woman who owned the home that I smoke bombed wanted to happen. She wanted to scare me out of making poor decisions. I found this out when I finally got picked up from jail by a family friend. The police told us that the homeowner did not want to press any charges or take legal action of any kind. She had made this decision even before they carried me off to jail. But the actual arrest and brief imprisonment was her plan. She told them to arrest me, take me to jail, fingerprint me, and show me what a life of poor decisions can lead to. So the whole process was more of a lesson (although a *huge* one) than anything else.

So no criminal record. No court appearance. No community service or monetary fines for my family. Just extreme remorse, embarrassment, and the terrifying experience of being a prisoner for three hours. Then there was the prevailing thought of what could have resulted from what I intended to be a simple joke. Someone's home could have burned down. Someone could have been killed. The reality of this extremely poor choice had begun to weigh on me. I absolutely hated that feeling. All of this added up to one concrete decision: *Never again.*

Chapter 5

THE "REAL" LORD OF MY LIFE

One weekend morning that fall, I had been sleeping on the living room couch when I was jarred out of my sleep by a persistent knocking on our apartment door. My mother opened the door, and it was the police. They asked if my second-oldest brother was in the house. My mother told them that he was upstairs sleeping. They went upstairs, made him get dressed, handcuffed him, and took him away. Just to buy more time with him, my mother asked the police if they would at least allow him to wash up. They said no. They walked out with my brother and left my mother crying. This hurt and was hard to watch.

She looked up at me and said, "Had I known they were coming for him, I would have told him to jump out of the window and run." My mother had a bad habit of taking full blame for things like this. My eldest brother was already doing time. She always felt a sense of guilt, and I understand it. I just hated to see her blame herself so completely.

Watching the cops arrest one of my family members was not new to me. But I was tired of it. It was the same horrible feeling each time. I would watch them get carried off to prison; then the usual would happen. Sadness and tears. Just an overall bad feeling would come over my entire household. For me, it started to feel like a curse. It was as if all of us were destined for jail. It felt inevitable, almost normal. Like a rite of passage. If you were a male in my family, you must drop out of school at some point, commit a crime, and go to jail. I was the youngest, getting close to my teen years, which was right about the time it started. The little smoke bomb jail incident was just a warning for me, but if I wasn't careful, it could also be a warm-up. My brother being carried off this time was extremely painful, for he would not return for the next nine years. I hated seeing that this was becoming all too common, and I refused to be next in line.

Later that same day, I went outside alone, walking around thinking about what I was going to do with myself. I didn't have any ideas. I didn't really know to seek God's help, as my relationship with him wasn't that deep yet. I only thought about God on Sundays at church. This was an "outside of church" issue (at least that's how my young mind processed it). As I walked around the neighborhood, I saw the usual. The drug dealers taking their posts. A few little kids playing in the grass. A stray dog or two running by. Someone playing loud music. The ice cream truck coming and going. Just the same old mundane things that happened on any other day.

Moments later, I would see something that I hadn't seen before in my life. I looked up and saw one of my friends dressed in a full football uniform. Helmet, shoulder pads—the whole thing. He played for the local city youth football team.

This blew me away because I *loved* football. We played neighborhood football all the time, and I was one of the best. But I never knew that there were organized youth football leagues for sixth graders to play. Seeing him dressed in full gear, looking just like the NFL teams looked, did something to me. I sprinted over to his mother's minivan and began to ask so many questions. My friend told me that anybody who lived in the city could play. I asked if I could check out a practice with him, and his mom agreed to take me along.

During the ride to the park where the team practiced, I had forgotten all about my brother. Not in a negative way. In a good way. It was so stressful, and I was so young, that it was probably a good thing that I had something else to think about. As my friend continued to talk to me about the daily practices, the cheerleaders, the game schedules, the crowds with all the parents, the trophies, and the team picnics—I was sold. I knew I wanted to be a part of this team before we even arrived. I almost didn't care what it looked like or how good the team was. It all just sounded like so much fun. He told me that he had been playing for a few years already, and after hearing all the stories, I could understand why he looked forward to it each year. It sounded amazing.

The park where the team practiced was only about four miles from our neighborhood. As we approached the park, I could see all the players assembling. Twenty to twenty-five other kids were all dressed in full football uniforms the same as my friend. They all looked just alike! A *team*. A real team. This was actually organized football for kids my age. I was blown away. I saw the coach walking around with a "Warrensville Bobcats" T-shirt on with his whistle and clip board. This stuff was legit! When we pulled into the parking lot, my heart started beating so fast. I had so much nervous energy, and I didn't even know why. I wasn't practicing or anything like that. Or *was I*...?

When we got out of the van, I sat on the side to watch. I listened to the coach call the players together with a loud blow of his whistle. He had on jogging pants, a tight T-shirt, and a yellow "Bobcats" hat. "Take a knee," he told the group. All the kids went down on one knee surrounding the coach. While he talked to them about the upcoming season, and about practices, and about keeping their grades up, and eating right...I felt like he was talking to *me*. I was listening to every word. I loved everything about this situation. The positive influence. The discipline. The togetherness. The colors of the uniforms. The smell of the grass. The way it made me feel.

As the coach kept laying out the plans, I grew more and more anxious about being a part of this team. Finally, he finished his speech and blew the whistle rapidly a few times. Quickly, all the players jumped up and ran away in a cluster that evolved into a long, flowing line as they began their usual warm-up laps. A few assistant coaches kept their eyes on the players as they ran to the far side of the field while the head coach walked over to his vehicle with a bunch of papers in his hands. He got close enough to me that I could introduce myself. So I did. Then I immediately told him that I wanted to play. He said I could, but I would need to bring him back a permission slip first. These were the papers that he had in his hand. I took one. I took two in case I lost one. I told him I would for sure bring him back a signed permission slip.

Before he walked away, I got bold. I asked if I could practice with them. He said no because if I got hurt, he would get into trouble. I had no equipment, so that made sense. What was I even thinking? (I told you, I was extremely excited.) I begged him to let me participate in some form. There had to be something that I could do. He decided to let me participate in the individual non-contact drills. All they did in this case was run sprints against each other, do some agility drills with cones and bags, and catch passes. In a sense, this felt like an opportunity to show what I could do. And I did just that. I put all that nervous energy to good use. I tore it up. Once the individual stuff ended, I had to take a seat. But I knew I wanted to play on this team, and I could tell the head coach now felt the exact same way. He had that "this boy better come back with that permission slip" look on his face. Meanwhile, I'm sitting there thinking, *I hope my momma say I can play on this team!*

On the ride home from the practice, the only thing I could think about was potentially playing in a real football game. I loved this team already, and I knew the coach liked me a lot. But the main person who needed to like the idea was my mother. When I got home, I begged my mother to let me play. She easily and quickly said yes, almost without question! I was *pumped.* She asked what I needed to do. I gave her the permission slip that had now somewhat turned into a paper airplane with all the folds in it. She read it with a smile, and I was smiling, too, of course. Then she suddenly frowned up a bit. She read that there was a $250 fee to play, and of course we couldn't afford it. Now my smile went to a frown too. I knew it was all over. We never could afford expensive stuff like that if it were not a 100 percent necessity. "Maybe next year, Lord's will," she said. She felt terrible, but I understood. I had grown accustomed to hearing those words: "We don't have the money for that, baby." I understood, but that doesn't mean I liked it at all. I didn't. In fact, I hated it.

The next day I saw my friend at the same time getting into the van, heading off to practice. I walked over to his front yard and told him the bad news. It was a no-go for me. He asked why, and I told him. His mother overheard me. She felt bad for me and said, "Well, it looks like I'll be paying two fees this year." I couldn't believe what I had heard. She told me to let my mother know that she would pay the fee. For context, I should note that this was one of my closer friends, and our parents knew each other. But we were not *that* close, meaning, nothing like this had ever happened between them. So while I was surprised at the gesture, I was also extremely grateful.

Now I was able to play for the city team and, *man,* did I make the most of it. I absolutely tore it up. For the next two years straight, I cared about nothing else but playing on this team. And when I say this, I mean that it was all I cared about, thought about, and dreamed about. I was always reading football books and magazines. If I wasn't reading about it, I was watching it. If I wasn't watching, I was drawing it. If I wasn't drawing it, I was playing it on a video game.

I remember when I first experienced a Cleveland Browns game. The crowd was *so loud.* Funny thing is, I was not a part of that crowd. I was on the outside of the stadium. I couldn't afford a Brown's game ticket. We just so happened to be running an errand in downtown Cleveland. But I will never forget the sound of the crowd roaring so loud that it felt like I was in there. I wanted to be in there. I knew better than to ask anybody to take me to a game. I already knew what the answer would be, and I understood the situation. But the continuing roar of that crowd began to spark something in me. Forget going to a game. I want to be *in* the game. I made a goal in my mind and heart that day that the best way to get to a Brown's game would be to play on the team myself. That day, my dream of becoming a pro football player started to take root.

Within those same two years featuring my newfound success and strong passions for organized football, my personal life still didn't change much. I still experienced the usual frustrations of life, only now I had something that gave me joy. Peace. Friends. Relevance. Purpose. More important than all of this, it gave me a way out. I was beginning to dream big and dream often: *Maybe I could go to college to play football and escape this dangerous environment. Maybe I could get drafted into the NFL one day and take care of my entire family.*

Football was giving me passion. Fire. I was beginning to write down goals and plan out the right moves I needed to achieve them. Football was maturing me. I wasn't afraid, intimidated, or doubtful that I could make this dream a reality. Football was making me courageous. It was strengthening me. It gave me a reason to get up every day with a positive attitude. The more I thought about using football to get to college and the NFL, the easier it became to force my *maybe* thoughts into *definitely* thoughts. I made up in my mind that I was going to make it, and I would let absolutely nothing stop me. Failure was not an option. The plan was non-negotiable. I was determined. Focused. Football was turning me into a go-getter. A hard worker. Football was giving me everything I needed. It became all I thought about. All I cared about. All that mattered, and the one thing I completely centered everything else around. Football. Football. Football. You know what football had unknowingly become? Idolatry. Football had become *lord of my life.*

You might be thinking that my dedication to football wasn't such a bad thing, especially since so many positive actions and thoughts birthed from my infatuation with the sport. I would agree with you. But the problem arises when a positive idea takes the place of God in our lives. This is what was happening to me as a young teenage ball player. I didn't fully know what it was like to make Jesus the center of everything or the foundation of my life. I wasn't taught to give my goals, dreams, desires, and passions to the Lord and let him decide what happens next. No, I best understood God as someone you take along for the ride. You pray for food, energy, strength, safety, touchdowns, and wins! But not for permission. Not about purpose. Those things were foreign to me in relation to my faith.

So I would set my goals based on whatever I wanted and then pray to Jesus to give me what I thought I needed to achieve them. I'd try to choose positive goals that made me feel good. It was not bad spiritually or a horribly wrong way to pray for a kid my age. At least I was praying. At least I had enough sense to know what God could do and where to put my trust. But it still wasn't right. Jesus didn't have first place in my life. That was football's spot.

But football at the center of my life stole God's glory. I was crediting football for everything good in my life and trusting it to open up so many opportunities. Spiritually, this was not sustainable. Of course, I didn't know how to worry about my spiritual well-being. That was too deep for me back then. But let's look at what I needed to consider: *What happens if I break a leg? What happens if I do not make it to college and I have to stay in my environment and live the tough life I'd become accustomed to?* If football was the center of my life, the only thing I cared about, and then for whatever reason it fails me—I'd then be left with this huge void. But if Jesus is always the center, then there is never a void. So whether I am in college playing football or in the ghetto experiencing a tough life—Jesus never changes. He never fails. He's always there and capable of carrying me through. That means no matter what I go through, if I allow Jesus to lead me, I'll never fail. That's why he needs to always be the center. Sounds so good to say these things now, at age forty-three. But at age thirteen or fourteen, nope. I didn't think like this. I hadn't learned to yet.

I innocently carried this train of thought throughout my high school years: Top priority—football. Everything else supports this goal. From the seventh grade on up to my senior year in high school, I dominated the sport as a running back. Soon I began to receive recruitment letters from several colleges, eventually settling on the University of Louisville. This was huge. It meant four important things: First, I would become the first male in my family to graduate high school. Second, I would become the first person in my family to attend college. Third, I could leave the dangers of my neighborhood, get out from under what felt like a curse, and start a new legacy of success. And fourth, I would be playing college football with a chance to go to the NFL and help my family.

I'm sure you can imagine my happiness when I signed that college scholarship. Now imagine the look on my face when the University of Louisville called me a few weeks later—*to cancel it.* My grades and ACT test scores were too low and did not get cleared by the NCAA. All scholarships were contingent upon clearing this process. The call from Louisville was the worst news of my life. I put the phone down and cried. And just like that, I went from having everything I wanted to having absolutely nothing.

Devastated doesn't do justice to describe how I was feeling that day. I was depressed. I was embarrassed. So many people had just watched me sign my scholarship, and now I would end up sitting right back on the corner with everyone else talking about "what could've been" or how I "almost had it." No. I refused. There had to be a way. I didn't know exactly what it could be, but there had to be something. While I tried to figure it out, I knew I needed something to do. I was eighteen years old and out of school with no plan.

I decided to get a job and quickly found one at a fast-food place. I hated it and quit it about a week later. All it did was remind me of my failure. Not that there is anything wrong with working at a fast-food place. A job is a job. But it felt different to me because just a week prior to flipping burgers,

I was riding the high of graduation and on my way to playing big-time college football at Louisville. This all came crashing down, and my thoughts were centered on the fact that burger flipping every day wasn't the best way to get the NFL's attention. So it was a depressing experience each day that I showed up for work.

Quitting my fast-food job only led to a different kind of depression. Now I was jobless and broke. With nothing to do, all I could think about was losing my scholarship. I knew I had to do something different. I immediately went out and found a different job, something that I felt would be much more pleasing to do. I figured I'd pick something that would allow me to help people, which is a great way to take your mind off yourself. I decided to go and apply for a job working with kids at the local YMCA.

They hired me as their new youth sports director. I felt so much better doing this job. I was still very much hurt about losing my scholarship, but working with these forty or fifty kids every day would take my mind off my troubles for a while. Some of these kids had rough childhoods, the same as I did. Some of them dreamed of playing on an NBA team. And, of course, some of them wanted to go to the NFL. And although it was a sports camp, they had all kinds of dreams, goals, and cool aspirations. I thoroughly enjoyed giving them encouragement each day, talking about what hurdles or roadblocks were getting in their way. Conversations like these always led to the same conclusion: *hang in there and don't quit.* One day I went back home after work with a simple thought: *Maybe I should take my own advice.*

I started to do my research to try and figure out what my options were. I was a high school graduate with a football scholarship offer on the table that I could not accept because my GPA and ACT scores were too low. I could not have been the only one in the world who had found him or herself in this situation. I knew there had to be something that I could do. I ended up discovering that junior college was an option. There were a few junior colleges that would give me a two-year scholarship, which would allow me to get my grades up and then transfer to a major university. Apparently, this was something that I could do right away, and there were several junior colleges who were willing to take an athlete like me.

Initially, I was extremely excited. But then, I just started to shake my head. I did not want to give up *two* of my four collegiate playing years. The ultimate goal for me was to get into the NFL, so I felt that every year of playing college football afforded to me was crucial. What if I were to get hurt? What if I didn't start right away? With only two years to play, that would make getting to the NFL much harder and less likely. So although junior college was a viable option, it was not the one for me.

As I continued to go back and forth to work over the summer, I kept researching more options and just held out hope that something would go my way. Finally, something did. I got a phone call from my recruiting coach from the University of Louisville. He informed me that there was a way in which they could reoffer me my scholarship. It would not be easy, but it would be possible—if I had what it takes to get it done. The recruiter told me that if I were able to raise my ACT test score by four points (from a seventeen up to a twenty-one), that an NCAA clearinghouse would allow me to enroll at Louisville on a full football scholarship. I smiled from ear to ear! I had no idea if I would be able to pull this off, but I was just happy to have a chance. The coach told me that I had until the end of the year to get this done. If I could not meet these requirements, unfortunately, they would have to move on. I told him that I was not letting them go anywhere.

Honestly, I had no clue how to get myself prepared enough to score a twenty-one on the ACT. College preparation was foreign to my family. I went back to my high school and discussed options with my counselors. Thankfully, my counselors at Bedford High School knew exactly what to do. They gave me information on how to sign up for ACT prep courses. I took all their advice and information and immediately got to work. I would work all day and study all night. Eventually, test day arrived. And I failed. I scored eighteen. I was dejected. And I felt like this test was just too hard. If all the studying I did raised my score by just *one* point and nearly blew my brain, then getting three more points was just going to be impossible. Thankfully, that thought came and went very quickly. There was no time to start whining and complaining. I immediately signed up to retake the test.

A few weeks later, test day number two arrived. Along with it was failure number two: a score of nineteen. I signed up for another retake. And failed again. This time, a score of seventeen. I was starting to go the wrong way, and my confidence began to follow. Time was running out, and so were my hopes.

I cried. Then I prayed. Better late than never. God already knew my heart. But I proceeded to tell him that I just did not want to fail. I asked him, *Why did I always have to lose?* I was pretty much out of ideas. So I promised God that if he would get me through this, I would do my very best to make the most of it. I would help as many people as I could. I would make something of myself. I begged him to show me a way.

I signed up to take the test for the fourth time. I was hoping for a miracle. A week later I got a call from the University of Louisville. My recruiting coach told me that he had some bad news. He went on to say that, unfortunately, if I had any plans for next fall, I need to cancel them—because I was going to be playing college football at the University of Louisville! I *screamed*. I cried. I couldn't believe it. My coach told me that I got the twenty-one that I needed. A few days later the actual test score results came in the mail. I was able to open up my scores for myself, and that big beautiful twenty-one was staring right back at me. I just dropped to my knees and started thanking God. I cried more. I had done it. I was on my way. And while I thanked God with my mouth, I think my heart was still saying: *Football, you have done it yet again.*

I Forgot

When I arrived at the University of Louisville, I completely left Cleveland behind in my mind and heart. All my struggles, disappointments, failures, and anything else negative, I worked as hard as I could to forget and put all my focus on being the best collegiate athlete. But in this process, I also made the unintentional error of forgetting about God.

When I was begging God to help me pass the ACT and get into college, I had told him that I would do everything I could to make sure that he was the Lord of my life. I wasn't quite sure that I knew what I was saying. It was something that I had heard in church, and I knew that this was the position that he was supposed to have in my life. But I did not know what having Jesus as Lord meant exactly. Sure, I had a few religious habits that I would stick to. In my mind, this was good enough. I went to church on Sundays. I went to some of the campus Bible studies. Sometimes I would lead one of them. I would even go and speak to young kids about Jesus. So I really thought that I was keeping up my end of the bargain.

But when I wasn't doing these good, God-honoring, spiritual things, I was lusting after girls, listening to explicit music, watching inappropriate movies, using bad language, and many other common (but sinful) behaviors that I did not think God cared about. But he very much cared. And whether I knew it or not, I absolutely was not honoring my promise to let Jesus be Lord. God still did not have first place in my life, and after two years of college, he decided to let me know about it.

When It Hit Me

God's timing is so amazing. He knew that I had yet to realize that I had made football the true lord of my life. My sophomore year of college, I broke my ankle in practice. I was going to be out of commission for several weeks, missing most of the season. I do not think it was a coincidence at all that God would use this time to teach me a lesson that would change my life forever.

In a Bible study with a student in my dorm room, I found out what it truly meant for Jesus to be the Lord of my life. As we sat one on one, this student told me that he had been watching me for several weeks. Because I was known around campus as a solid Christian, he took interest since that was a rare thing to see from star athletes. But what this student was seeing in my life did not reflect the actions of a person who followed Jesus wholeheartedly.

He proceeded to tell me that he had seen me consistently lusting after girls on campus. He heard me blasting the explicit lyrics and music from my car. He heard me many times use profanity and laugh at dirty jokes. He then showed me Scripture verse after Scripture verse after Scripture verse that spoke against doing such things. I had never really paid attention to the Scriptures before. The result of this Bible study was a life-changing spiritual revelation for me. I realized that it was not okay for Jesus to be only my Savior; he must also be my Lord. And for him to be Lord, I must live in obedience to him. His way, not my own.

This hit me like a ton of bricks. All I could do was cry. I didn't care who was around. I felt so bad. God had done so much to get me to college. More than that: God had done so much to get me through life! And the way that I was saying thank you was by living a life satisfying to only myself—but not Jesus. I was crushed. Scriptures such as Matthew 7:21–23 really grabbed my attention:

> Not everyone who says to me, "Lord,
> Lord," will enter the kingdom of
> heaven, but only the one who does the
> will of my Father who is in heaven. Many
> will say to me on that day, "Lord, Lord,
> did we not prophesy in your name and in
> your name drive out demons and in your
> name perform many miracles?" Then I will
> tell them plainly, "I never knew you. Away
> from me, you evildoers!" (NIV)

Instantly, the most important thing to me became pleasing God—not myself. And now that I was aware of what the Bible said and what God expected of me, I could no longer say, "I didn't know God cared." After looking over several convicting Scripture passages, I now knew exactly what it truly meant to have Jesus be Lord of my life. Not only did I realize that I had put football in the place where Jesus needed to be, I also learned from Scripture how to allow and use the Holy Spirit to help me replace my sport with my God—*and keep it that way*.

I might have become a believer in Jesus when I was about seven years old. But it wasn't until that day—my sophomore year at the University of Louisville—that I transitioned from being just a believer in Jesus to a true follower. From then on, whenever I read Scripture, I would do so with purpose. I threw away all the trashy music and movies. I made it my goal to stop lusting after women, and I began praying for a wife. I cleaned up my language and many of my bad habits. Whenever I failed at doing any of the above, I deeply repented and did everything I could to turn away from whatever sin had knocked me down. I would go on to face many more challenges during my final two years of college. That's another story altogether. But just know this: my time at the University of Louisville may have been the most important years of my life. It's when and where I learned to put Jesus first. There will never be a greater lesson learned, and for that I am immeasurably grateful.

Chapter 6

LEVETTE

My junior year in college was a very pivotal year for me. I was getting close to graduation as well as to the NFL draft. Of the many goals that I had set for myself during my childhood, one of them was realized the summer after my sophomore year, just after I had learned to put Jesus in his proper place as Lord of my life. I knew that one of the weakest parts of my faith was lust, and I wanted to root out that sin. There was only one way to do this in a God-honoring way. Get married.

This was not my first thought about marriage. I actually proposed to a girl when I was eighteen years old. I had just graduated high school, still learning what true love was, and I thought we were in it together. I was only months away from heading to Louisville on my football scholarship, and I had heard that girls really chased after football players on campus. My recruitment visit confirmed that warning to be true. Believe it or not, I did not want that kind of attention. I had nearly lost the scholarship already, and I figured girl-chasing would not be wise right off the bat. I wanted to be focused on my academics.

So I figured already having a solid relationship would be a great idea and would eliminate the desire to seek out partying and girls. I remember saving up a few hundred dollars from my part-time job at the local YMCA in Bedford, Ohio, and purchasing the best engagement ring I could find. I was broke after that, but I thought she was definitely worth it. She was shocked at my proposal—but said yes! Then months into the engagement, some fella with a lot more cash than me pretty much stole her away through constant gifts that I couldn't match. When a mutual friend alerted me of this gifting relationship, I called her on the phone and confronted her about it. She claimed nothing was going on and that he was an old acquaintance who still had an attraction to her—but she only stayed in contact with him because of the gifts.

I listened as she presented her case. He didn't mean much to her; it was all about the presents for her. Fair enough—but *no*. I wasn't willing to accept that. She pushed back, as if I was being irrational. Now I was offended. So I promptly gave my then fiancée an ultimatum: "It's gotta be either the gifts or me—one has to go." *She chose the gifts!* Of course, at that point, I ended the relationship, slamming the phone down in anger. The fiancé life and the marital plans would have to wait.

As the time to head off to school got closer, I still had the goal of getting into a meaningful relationship, but not an engagement. I met a nice girl about a month before leaving for college. It probably wasn't ideal to start a new relationship with someone and allow strong feelings to develop knowing that I'd be leaving the state in just a few weeks. But we were having such a good time being together that neither of us thought the distance would matter. But after I left, it wasn't long before the stress of maintaining an out-of-state relationship took its toll. She called me to tell me that she couldn't do it anymore. She gave up. Writing her name on my taped wrists so that she could see it on TV when I played apparently didn't do the trick. The distance quickly killed the relationship after two short months.

Nevertheless, I kept the goal of trying to find the right love. She had to be out there somewhere. I continued dating throughout college, and with each new relationship, I wondered if she was going to be the one. But as time passed, none of these relationships would stick. I started to think that maybe I wasn't meant to get too tight with anybody else until after college. But the idea of being in a committed relationship excited me much more than being single. I couldn't help what was deep inside my heart. I was in search of my life partner. That special lady who would be my best friend. At the same time, I was getting so tired of hopping from woman to woman, having super high hopes, only to see it eventually come to an end.

I was worn out from relationships. Then a funny thing happened. Let me preface this by making a suggestion to you: Just because something works when you try it doesn't mean it is the right thing to do. A risk taken that ends up panning out doesn't justify or validate the risk. Sometimes it's just a product of something going your way at that moment in time. But that doesn't guarantee that God had anything to do with it. That is why prayer is so important. Prayer helps ensure that our moves in life are God-led.

Which brings me to what I did next. My *fed-up-ness* with meeting new girls led to what I thought was a more common-sense approach. I decided to seek something more familiar: my high school sweetheart. We had dated in high school and lost touch after that. I decided to type her name in a search, thinking that if I actually found her, then it had to be fate. Well, I found her! We connected. She even drove to my college so that we could have a serious talk about a plan of action for our future. Well, I'll spare you the details, but once again, what I thought was a good plan failed.

The relationship treadmill was getting old, discouraging, and exhausting. It seemed that I was too serious for the time of life that I was in. I don't think many of these women thought as far down the road about life and love as I was thinking. I didn't know if I would ever find a woman who was at the same stage of life as I was and who viewed relationships the way I did. I was looking for a life partner—not a girlfriend. Maybe it was time to re-evaluate that. I didn't know. But it was definitely time to stop trying to look up old flames or hoping to get lucky or rewarded by "fate." That much was clear. Honestly, I started not to care, and I was close to just giving up altogether on the whole idea of "finding the one." I had tried everything, and I felt like it was time to stop trying.

However, there was one thing that I had not done. There was something that I had recently learned how to do, which was to pray specifically and intentionally about what I wanted. More importantly, I needed to ask God about who *he* wanted me to have. Big difference there. What would happen if I seriously just humbled myself and asked God for *his choice*?

I pondered that thought hard. Who did he want me to spend the rest of my life with? Straight up begging God to reveal the woman of his choosing—in *his* timing—was something I hadn't done yet. This might have been why I was trapped on the dating carousel. I decided it was time to change that. I truly had faith that something would come out of this authentic act of faith and trust in God, so prayers went up aggressively and specifically.

The spring before my junior year at college, I specifically prayed for a woman who would be focused on loving God as much as I was trying to. A woman who would be committed to me in ways unimaginable. A woman who wanted to start a family and raise them to be Christ followers. A woman who would always challenge me to be the absolute best man that I could ever be and would also never cease to hold me accountable to the Lord. I simply told God what I thought this woman might be like. What I thought I truly needed. Bottom line, I just wanted whomever *he* had for me. His choice. I gave him my heart. Then I simply focused on living my life while waiting in faith.

Months later, the wait ended. In response to my plea, God led me to Levette Robinson, who would eventually become my wife—the beautiful Levette Stallings. But believe me when I tell you that God must have an awesome sense of humor because my road to meeting Levette and capturing her heart *was a trip.*

Computer Love?

Summer 2000. I was sitting in the student computer lab passing time on what was then a popular online college chat room. Students from all over the world could talk to each other, share photos, or even exchange phone numbers (in private chat rooms) if it ever got that far. Admittedly, things were not always appropriate in these chat rooms. I had already started my account my freshman year, so my standards for spiritual cleanliness had matured exponentially by my junior year. I was close to deleting my account and moving on because I began to feel that there was really no need to continue exposing myself to the temptation.

I figured that this would be my last week logging on and was enjoying the appropriate parts of the experience as best I could. I had met some cool people from all around the country. One person in particular was Levette, a beautiful college basketball player at Morehead State University. As I was scrolling, suddenly I got a "pop up" speech bubble on my screen that said, "Hey!" Levette was sending me an instant message. We decided to slide off into a private chat room to continue our discussion.

Levette and I had been chatting off and on, but due to her basketball schedule, we hadn't talked most of the winter or spring. We had quite a bit to catch up on, so our discussion turned into a long, enjoyable back and forth. A friend of mine walked up behind me and looked over my shoulder. He asked me if I was talking to Vette Robinson. I looked at him like he had two heads, wondering how he knew her name because all that was showing up was her picture and the transcript of our conversation. He let me know that he and Levette went to high school together. Now this was news to me because I had no idea that Levette was a local! I honestly had never read her profile, and I assumed Levette lived somewhere clear across the country. When it came to her location, the only question I had asked referred to what school she attended. I had never heard of Morehead State University, so I still didn't know where she lived. I didn't really care anyway—I just knew that she was beau—ti—ful. It didn't matter to me if she lived on the moon. Nonetheless, it was good that her high school friend was with me because she began asking him all kinds of questions about me (and I was asking him a ton of questions about her). Once we both were satisfied with the answers that we got, we agreed to meet in person. It turns out that all this time, Levette and I had only been about twenty minutes away from each other. I had been sitting there chatting with her online thinking she lived thousands of miles away, and yet I could have gone to her house on foot if I wanted to.

We agreed to meet that same day, so we exchanged numbers, and she gave me the address to her home. Levette had just graduated from Morehead with a bachelor's degree in industrial engineering and technology. Her plan was to take some time off before starting her career, so she still lived comfortably with her parents and younger brother.

When I logged off the computer and began to prepare to go and meet Levette, I knew there was a chance that I could be meeting my future wife. This might seem like my thought process was very premature, but it wasn't. It was right in line with my prayers. I knew that I was no longer looking for just another girlfriend. At this point, I wasn't even looking for a potential best friend. I was looking for my answered prayer, and I was hoping she was the one. This hope dictated a lot of the decisions I made in my preparations to go meet Levette. I decided not to get all fancy dressed. I kept on my workout clothes. I just wanted to be raw and real and hoped that she would be the same.

When I arrived at her home, I saw a beautiful girl sitting on the hood of a car backed in her driveway. To make sure this was Levette, I double checked the address. When I saw that I had the right address, I was also able to see that she sure did have *a lot* of protection with her. Levette's mother, father, brother, and rottweiler were all on the porch watching. I got so nervous that I actually kept driving past the house even though I knew I had the right one.

After composing myself, I made the U-turn, drove back to her home, and introduced myself. She was just as beautiful in person as she was online. Just like me, she was dressed in athletic clothes. She went on to explain to me that she hoped I wasn't expecting her to get all dolled up because she was not that kind of girl. She reminded me that she loved to play basketball and liked to sweat, and whoever wanted to date her needed to be okay with that.

Already we were off to a good start because that's exactly how I felt. As we continued to talk and it was clear that we were on the same page, I asked her what she wanted to do for our first date. She said basketball. I was thinking she wanted to go see a basketball game, but no—she wanted to go play. Against me. One on one. She insisted that this be the first date. No lunch, dinner, movie, bowling, walk in the park—nothing like that. It had to be basketball first. I thought she was weird—but she was too beautiful to disagree with, so I said okay.

So Glad I Got Serious

The next day I went to pick Levette up and take her to my college campus for our little game. As we were walking inside the gym, I asked her if she was sure she really wanted to do this for the first date. She said, "Absolutely," and headed into the women's locker room. I shook my head and went to go change as well. When I came back out to the gym floor, she was already there and going through a serious warmup. I just laughed a little bit to myself. I thought maybe she just wanted to see if I had a problem with my girlfriend being a sweaty athlete. I wasn't sure why we were here. But I didn't care. Whatever the reason, I was up for it—because she was beautiful, and I absolutely loved how athletic she was. I walked up to her and we briefly hugged. Almost immediately she said to me, "You ready?" The way she said it was almost cryptic. I said, "Yeah, let's go."

SWISH. Right off the bat, she *drained* a long jumper. I thought it was cute and simply laughed it off. In a very playful and flirtatious way, I complimented the fact that she had a nice shot. I was smiling, flashing those pearly whites. But her pearly whites were just chomping down on her gum, eyes focused like she was in the WNBA finals. On her next possession, she drained another long jumper. She said, "That's two.

Game's ten. You better get serious." I'm thinking to myself, *Okay—you want to* for real *play*. Because by now she was starting to talk a lot of trash! So on her third possession, I figured I better humble her a little bit. I backed off a few extra feet so that she would be tempted to shoot yet another long jumper. Only this time I was going to smack that ball clear across the gym floor. Sure enough, she went for the jumper, and I skied in the air for the block—but it was a pump fake. She easily made a lay-up, and I just stood there looking stupid. She smiled and called out the score: three to zero.

At this point, I was actually kind of mad. It was time to get serious. (Three points too late, of course, but I digress.) On her next possession, I got a steal, and then things got real. We went back and forth. Point for point. I somehow ended up winning this game 10 to 9. Levette walked up to me, looked me in my face, and with the most beautiful smile you have ever seen, she said: "You lucky you won because I don't date guys that I can beat in basketball."

I wanted to marry her right there where she stood.

Of course, I did not marry her that day. I had only known her two days, and had I botched this basketball game, it would have ruined the opportunity for there to be a third. But fortunately for me, I won our little game, which won me another (more conventional) date. And we continued to date for three months, fell deeply in love, and got engaged. We were married nine months later, on June 9, 2001. We had our first child a year later, a beautiful baby girl, and six years later she would give birth to our son.

This family was the one I prayed for. My loving wife and our two children would represent the continual breaking of generational curses. At the time of the writing of this book, I am in the eighteenth year of a fantastic, beautiful, purposeful, fulfilling, God-led, Christ-centered, Holy Spirit-filled marriage. And to think, I almost let Satan influence my marriage. Before my relationship with Levette became this beautiful thing that it is now, Satan attacked us constantly—especially me.

The first year, I struggled with fear. As a married man still in college with no training in being a family man, having never raised a family before, and having never been financially responsible for anyone other than myself, I became afraid. Satan tried to capitalize on that fear by tempting me to ask for a divorce. I thought about it all the time during the first year. I figured that I would end it before it really got going. I thought we rushed into it, or maybe I rushed *her* into it.

While dealing with these fearful thoughts, there was also the temptation to flirt with other women, being a still-maturing college senior. But God warned me in multiple ways that what I thought was harmless, college fun was really like playing with fire. It was also hurting Levette. Hugging people for too long, flirting on social media, and other seemingly insignificant actions could easily escalate if not kept in check. So we kept them in check. Because I seemed to struggle with this, my wife and I agreed that it would be best if I didn't have close female friends in college. This was absolutely the right thing to do, but at the time, I was just too "marriage immature" to understand the importance. I began to feel as though married life was handcuffing me. Suddenly, my unmarried teammates appeared to be having so much more fun than I was. The fact that they had many more options than I did was starting to bother me. My mind was trying to come up with any logical way out of that commitment that we made at the altar. Satan almost had me. Either my fear or flirtatiousness were at risk of going too far if God did not intervene quickly. But intervene he did.

Through Scripture I realized that these tempting thoughts and fears of inadequacy were Satan's way of trying to derail our union; they were not from God. I learned how to use the power of God to calm the fears and kill the temptation from anyone outside of my marriage before anything came close to destroying what God had built. I also began to consider my daughter, this newborn child who needed to grow up in something solid—not the divorce or brokenness that I was born into.

We knew better days were ahead, but we just needed to decide that it was worth it for both of us to see them *together.* We decided that life apart was not an option. Through prayer and the grace of God, I eventually developed a view of Levette that helped me come as close as possible to seeing her how Jesus does: precious and irreplaceable.

Thank you, Jesus—for sending me such a beautiful gift of a woman. (And thank you for leading me to quit the wrestling team while in high school, to practice my basketball skills, and to make that *team instead! Otherwise, years later, Levette would have mopped the floor with me!)*

Chapter 7

UNFULFILLED

On April 19, 2002, my daughter, Antonia Christian Stallings, was born. I had just finished my senior football season at Louisville. The 2002 NFL draft was held the day after my daughter was born. My daughter had a difficult birth and had to spend several days in the ICU. Meanwhile, Levette and I spent a couple nights in the recovery room.

Anxiety and tension for both of us were very high. Our daughter was recovering in one room, completely out of our sight, and on top of that, my phone was constantly ringing as my agent continued to update me on my status in the NFL draft. I had been projected by many to go in the fourth round. But instead, I was not drafted at all. This would have been a really hard pill to swallow had I been able to fully focus on the reality of not getting picked. But with my daughter still having trouble while in the ICU, my mind was fixed on her safety.

When my wife was finally able to leave recovery and go home, the hospital informed us that we would not be able to take our daughter home that day. Probably one of the toughest things that Levette and I have ever had to do was leaving that hospital without Christian. The drive back home to our apartment was tough as we looked in the rearview mirror at the empty car seat. Add to that a phone call from my agent saying that no NFL team was interested in signing me at the time. We tried hard to focus on the positives. As far as we knew, at least we were blessed by God with a beautiful baby girl. We just hoped that we could add the word "healthy" to that praise report as soon as possible.

Once we got home and settled in, we continued to struggle with the fact that our daughter was still not with us. Her crib was all set. The gifts from Levette's baby shower were still spread out all around the house. We talked to each other about many different things and tried to laugh as much as we could, but then, of course, we would think of Christian when everything got quiet again.

I would also think about my football career. By not getting drafted, I felt like a failure. I didn't have any other goals in my heart. There were no other aspirations, back-ups, or plan B's. I wasn't quite sure what to do next. Whether we were talking about our daughter's health or my football career, there were no answers available for either. For two days straight, we were separated from our baby. At the same time, I had no idea what I would do for work. Although it was my senior season athletically, I still had a semester of school left academically. I stopped going to class so that I could train for potential NFL free agent workout invites, but those invites never materialized.

Finally, after over forty-eight hours of waiting, the hospital told us we could come pick up our baby. Around the same time, I got a phone call from an arena football team that was willing to offer me a contract. My baby was happy and healthy, and I had a job playing football. It wasn't the NFL, but at least it was professional. At least it was an opportunity to keep playing football, which meant I could still possibly get a chance to show the NFL what I could do.

In 2002, I had a successful first year in the arena league. But this did not lead to any offers from the NFL or any other major football league. The arena league only paid about $200 per game. This amount could barely pay half of my rent at the time, let alone all the other bills. But my heart had been hardened towards giving up my pro football dreams. When it came to talk of giving in and settling for a more stable nine-to-five job, I never wanted to discuss it. And my pride would not allow me to give up my NFL goal just to start flipping burgers again, especially in the same city in which I was a college football star.

If I didn't do something, that meant that I was going to be doing nothing. And that's exactly what happened. I avoided jobs that I felt made me look stupid and embarrassed. I wasn't ready for that yet. Each day I focused on trying to figure out how to get into the NFL. I was constantly pressuring my agent, scouring the internet for some sort of opportunity, and pursuing other fruitless efforts every day. Not one NFL team was showing interest. I couldn't get any invites for a tryout of any kind. I was always checking for an email or exciting text. Nothing. All I did every day was stare at the phone waiting for my agent to call. These calls never came. And even when the phone did finally ring and I would get super excited, it would usually just be an update about not hearing anything yet. This eventually led to an extreme amount of frustration. It also led to a lot of late and overdue bills. And that eventually led to lights, gas, and power being cut off.

It was embarrassing. I probably could have asked for help at the time, but being in Louisville made doing so extremely hard. Not only was this the same city where I was a collegiate football star, but this was also the city where I played arena football as a pro. For four months, I was scoring touchdowns, signing autographs, and doing commercials. Then, only weeks later, I was supposed to go around the city looking for handouts and loans? I did not want the whole city to know that T.C. Stallings could not pay his rent and was now sitting in the dark with the electricity shut off. I didn't want to be a newspaper headline. I didn't want to hear any reporters saying on the local news that a former Louisville great was struggling to make ends meet.

This was the reality though. It was exactly what we were doing. Struggling. I remember being able to muster up enough cash to pay everything but the electric bill. It was so frustrating to have been able to buy food but not to be able to keep our refrigerator on to preserve it. Sobering doesn't begin to describe it. *What do I do?*

I was weighing all my options as I just sat there in the dark. Then, Levette and my daughter came into the room. This was significant because it reminded me of a very special moment. On this night, rather than complain, criticize, or worry, Levette placed two candles on the table to create some light and to brighten my mood. We lit the candles together, just like we did when we got married. We then pulled out Monopoly, one of our favorite board games, and started playing by candlelight. We laughed and had fun, and then we just prayed for better days.

I looked at Christian and knew I had to do better for her. Levette's parents had moved to Alabama, and when her dad gave her away to me in marriage, he did so with the understanding that I would always take care of her. I knew it was time to humble myself and make a meaningful move. As we prayed together, I knew I had to be ready to respond to God's answer, even if it meant doing something that I didn't want to do.

Back to...Cleveland

And...what do you know; God answered my prayers by leading me to do something I didn't want to do. Reluctantly, my struggles led me back to the place that I'd tried so hard to escape— Cleveland, Ohio. I was back living with my mother, now with a wife and daughter, and the plan was to stay there until I was able to get back on my feet. This was tough because my mom's apartment didn't have much room for guests, but it was so good to be with her again after so many years. I was also proud to have her meet Christian. Meanwhile, it was up to me to figure out a plan of action.

My agent continued to try to get me opportunities with NFL teams, and while he worked hard on that, I pursued employment. I began working two jobs simultaneously while trying to stay in shape in case a team would call. Levette ended up finding a part time job as well, and with all three incomes, we were able to finally get our own place to live. We found a house for rent in the inner city of Cleveland. This was not the safest place to live, but it was all that we could afford. It was also close to my childhood church, and of course, I started going back there again.

The latter part of 2002, I spent most of my time working two jobs and studying a lot of Scripture. Eventually, I started to feel a strong desire to enter ministry. On February 7, 2003, after several months of studying, I entered the ministry and taught my first message to a full congregation at Blessed Hope Missionary Baptist Church. From this point on, teaching people about Jesus became a very strong passion of mine. I would study Scripture every day and was often given the opportunity to preach and teach at churches around the city of Cleveland. If I was not teaching at a church, I was most likely at one of my two jobs.

I was so busy that I rarely had time to just sit and think. But when I did find time, all I could think about was how much I hated how hard life had become. I was living out my nightmare, which was being a man who lived a life that consisted of nothing but hard labor from nine-to-five in a job that I didn't like. And by the time I got home, I ate, slept, and repeated the cycle. I did not think that people chose that type of lifestyle but rather were forced into it. And I had always told myself, if I'm forced into it, then I will most certainly man up and do it, *but I would never choose it.* Other than teaching the Bible, I didn't love anything else that I was doing. But since I did not get paid to do ministry (nor did I expect to be), I was forced to do the work that I hated. I was living my nightmare—waking up each day constantly unfulfilled.

Finally?

One day out of nowhere I got some good news. My agent informed me that I had been invited to a few open workouts with the NFL. These types of workouts provided only a glimmer of hope at best because usually only one or two guys (out of hundreds in attendance) benefitted from them. But it still represented *a chance*. Some form of hope. Reluctantly, I had to quit one of my jobs in order to properly capitalize on this NFL tryout. In my mind, I absolutely had to do this. Yes, it was risky, and yes, it could potentially cause me to struggle with paying our bills, but there was no way that I could work both jobs all day—everyday—and still be prepared for a legit NFL tryout. Levette was understandably nervous about my quitting one of the jobs. But I begged her to just trust me. *Believe in me.* In hindsight, I should not have put that kind of pressure on her, but I looked at this workout as a once in a lifetime opportunity. I reminded her that these everyday odd jobs were not going anywhere, but this NFL opportunity might never come back again.

Levette knew how well I could play, but she was growing tired of the grind. She was getting weary from seeing my pain every time I got rejected. I was tired of seeing it too. We both were tired of struggling financially. But I still did not want to give up the pursuit. I refused to quit. I told her to let me worry about the bills, and I promised to address any shortages. I begged her to trust me and to know that I would use all our current struggles as motivation to try even harder at the workout. Levette was reluctant yet always my absolute biggest cheerleader. Other than my mother, nobody wanted me to succeed more than my wife. We prayed together, and she got behind me. She didn't agree to the workout to please me. She agreed because she believed in me. She knew that if given a fair opportunity, I would make an NFL team. She knew that I was headed to this workout with a mountain-sized chip on my shoulder and a desire that no scale could measure in weight. She knew that I would go and give it absolutely everything I had. I always did. And that's exactly what happened.

But neither team chose me.

After working out for two NFL teams and having neither of them give me a shot, I was dejected. Devastated. I started to wonder if God even wanted me to play football. I'd ask him all the time in prayer. Maybe all the teams rejecting me was his answer. I really wasn't sure what to do at this point. I started to feel confused and even a bit desperate. That might explain why I decided to do what I did next.

The Cleveland Browns

After neither of the two NFL teams that I worked out for decided to sign me, I was back to square one. I found another job, but we had already gotten severely behind with our bills. I needed to do something fast. So I got a crazy idea. I just grabbed my highlight tapes, drove down to Berea, Ohio, where the Cleveland Browns training facility was, walked right in with no appointment, and asked for a meeting with the running backs coach. They told me that he would be busy for most of the day and could not guarantee a time that he would be free. I told them that I was in no hurry, that I would be willing to wait all day if I had to.

They did not make me leave, and so the wait began. Even I was shocked when the running backs coach finally came out and sat with me. I kid you not—I got the meeting! He took me into his office, and we watched my highlight tape. He told me that I was very impressive. He said that they were already looking at a lot of running backs, but he would be willing to see if there was anything that he could do. For me, this was about as close as I had gotten too receiving a legit opportunity.

I remember going home and telling Levette that I think it is finally about to happen for me. She couldn't believe that I walked in unannounced and got a meeting. She wasn't the only one. I actually started to think that God was finally about to open that door that I had been trying to bust down for over two years.

The next few days at work were bittersweet. Bitter because I hated my jobs. Sweet because it was a lot easier to sit there and work knowing that at any moment, I could get a call from the Cleveland Browns. But several days went by, and I never got a call. My excitement and optimism started to diminish. Since it was a drastic measure that got me the meeting in the first place, I felt like another drastic measure wouldn't hurt.

So I went to the Browns website and found the team's directory page, and I literally called every single number on it. Every one. There wasn't a person in the Cleveland Browns facility that didn't get the same message on their voicemail.

The janitor even got a message. It didn't matter who they were, if I saw their name in that directory, then they got a message from running back T.C. Stallings. I just told them that if they gave me a shot, that this homegrown Cleveland man would give it everything he had. I told them that I didn't even have to be paid while in camp. I just wanted a shot to prove what I was worth. It was heartfelt. Short and to the point, but definitely heartfelt. My goal was for everyone in that facility to be talking to each other saying, "Did you get a weird message from a running back named T.C. Stallings?"

I am literally laughing right now as I am writing this story, but it wasn't a joke to me at all back then. I was going to bug them so much that they would have to give me a shot eventually or at least call me back and give me a tryout. This was the kind of thing that you see happen in movies, so maybe this could be my movie moment!

Twenty-four hours later, I was at work, and my cellphone rang. I looked at the caller ID—and it said, "Cleveland Browns." I could not believe it. My stomach dropped as if I were on a roller coaster. I knew that this was not a joke because I had the Cleveland Browns' number saved into my cellphone. I ran into the hallway to answer the call, excited to talk to the head coach, or the offensive coordinator, or the running backs coach, or any of the coaches—I didn't care. They all for sure got a message!

But the voice I heard did not come from anyone I wanted to talk to because it was the Cleveland Browns' police and security team. They told me to stop calling the facility, and if any of the coaches are interested, they would call me. They kindly advised me to never again blow up every single phone at their facility the way I did. Mortified, I gave them my word. All that excitement I had before the call had turned back into the familiar depressing feeling of unfulfillment.

I wasn't sure why football still had such a stronghold on my heart. Football wasn't the lord of my life anymore—Jesus definitely was. Now, I was just having a hard time hearing his voice and understanding his plans for me.

I Can't Do This

After the whole Cleveland Browns let down, it became hard to get motivated. But then, something exciting happened. It would require adding yet another job that didn't involve helmets and shoulder pads, but it did involve making more money, something I desperately needed. It was a unique situation that sounded extremely intriguing on the surface. It was a gig that paid $32.50 an hour, and it was a two hour per day job. That was $75 per day. I barely made that per day working eight hours. This sounded great.

The job was unloading bananas from a truck, which sounded easy enough. The catch was that the truck came between the hours of two and four in the morning. Now that's early, but even that didn't bother me too much. The total time commitment was about three hours, including travel and the gig itself. The thought of being able to *not* work all day and make the same amount of money was attractive. I knew I wouldn't like being on call from two to four in the morning each day, but if I wanted to free up my daytime hours for football training, this was the only way. I decided to do it.

The first day wasn't bad at all. I got the call, and I drove up to the loading dock in the middle of the night. I played my favorite jams to get me in the mood. I wanted to have a great attitude about this, so I kept reminding myself while sipping my coffee that it was just two hours. It had to end at some point. And this place paid $75 cash on the spot each day, so I didn't even have to wait for a check. I was excited. I felt blessed. It wasn't the easiest situation, but I felt like I had caught a break. And maybe, just maybe, by having my days to myself, I could stay in shape for a possible NFL chance. A real one, this time.

I arrived at the docks and met my trainer for the day. He explained to me that while the job was fairly simple, there was a precise way that it needed to be done. He also warned me that when dealing with these banana boxes, I needed to watch out for spiders that also sometimes make the trip. That put up some antennas. But I was okay. Apparently, everybody gets used to the spiders eventually. Suddenly the huge garage door went up, and the 18-wheeler started backing in. It was beeping and backing in, and I was saying to myself, *Man...these things are a lot bigger and longer than I thought.* My trainer popped the latch at the back of the truck, and it opened up with a roar, like a big manual garage door. And all I could see, wall to wall, floor to ceiling, were tightly packed banana boxes. Twenty-five hundred of them.

At first, I wasn't bothered because I just knew we'd be using a forklift for all these boxes. Nope. We had to hand-place these boxes in a certain order, in a certain design, on a single pallet, one at a time. Once we finished stacking them (about twenty-five on each pallet, four feet in height), *then a guy would come on a forklift and take the pallet away. I wanted his job.* My trainer showed me the pattern for stacking the boxes, and I joined in. He stayed with me the entire time, and just under two hours later, we were finished. This was back-breaking work, but the trainer and I had fun. It was a tough job but not too bad. Then they dropped that $75 in my hand, and the day was done. I felt like I could pull this off. I got home and went to sleep, then woke up around noon-ish. I actually was a bit too tired to take advantage of the day with some football training. Oddly, that really didn't bother me too much. I played with my daughter, talked with my wife, ate, watched TV. Next thing I knew, I was asleep. Then the phone rang at in the middle of the night. It was three in the morning, the call to alert me that the truck has arrived. This was the start of day two.

Day two was different in a way that I did not expect it to be.

First of all, I was extremely tired. I was not used to being snapped out of my sleep at two or three in the morning. Secondly, I had slept most of the day before, which made the day go much too fast. I was too tired to do anything else. All that banana box moving really took it out of me. Now, I had to do it all over again. I wasn't excited at all about day two. But I looked at my wife and daughter sleeping. I knew I had to go.

I grabbed my cup of coffee and hit the road. But this time, I wasn't in a music mood. I didn't care about getting hype. I knew exactly what the next couple of hours would consist of. Nothing to be hyped about. In fact, I was irritated.

All the sleeping from the previous day felt like a waste of precious time, and now I was right back in the car, headed to the docks for unloading. Even though it had been nearly a full twenty-four hours since I had unloaded my first truck, I felt like I was just there two hours ago. In the quiet of the car, I begin to think about my life. I started to wonder if this was all there would ever be for me. But as I pulled into the lot and saw the trucks lining up to be emptied, I shook off the feeling. I tried to look on the bright side. Two hours, and I'm out.

I signed in and walked down the corridor leading to my area. The garage door opened, and the truck backed in. They reminded me that I will not have a supervisor, and that all the unloading would be my responsibility alone. I opened the back of the truck and started the one-man job. I had my headphones on, listening to the same songs that I would use when training for football. I was working hard, and the sweat began to pour. This was a much harder gig when I was doing it alone. It was also very monotonous. Box after box after box. I took a water break about forty minutes in, and I had barely put a dent into those twenty-five hundred or so boxes. My lower back began to get tight and stiff. The job was taking forever due to my lack of proficiency with the stacking format. Some of the pallets I had to redo. Meanwhile, the music was a reminder of where I truly wanted to be. In a gym somewhere training for football. On a track running. Not slinging these boxes at three in the morning.

All of a sudden, reality hit me hard. I wrestled with the fact that something like this could end up being my life. This was it? This is what I went through three and a half years of college for? This is what I did all the football training for? Just to end up on the back of a truck, tossing boxes? After getting about halfway done, I started feeling bad. Like a failure. I started to feel like my life was getting away from me, and the banana truck unloading gig was a sign of things to come. I slammed a few more boxes into place, forming yet another monotonous four-foot-high pallet of bananas.

After putting the last box on top of the current pallet I had just completed, I looked around at what I was doing. I took a deep breath and just broke down a bit. A few tears started to fall. I took my headphones off. I put my head in my hands and cried on the boxes. No noise; just tears. I was hurting. I was frustrated. I was angry. It wasn't the work. Yes, the work was hard, but I could do it—*if I had to*. But I didn't think I *had to*. At least, *I shouldn't* have to. I knew I was better than this. I wasn't beneath the banana job, but I just felt that a job like this was something that I would take whenever or if ever there was absolutely nothing else that I was talented enough to do. And I felt like I was built for so much more.

I was in my early twenties. I was strong. Fast. Smart. In my eyes, it was too early in my life to settle down to unloading trucks as a career. It was nowhere near anything I ever wanted. I felt as though life was forcing me to go this route against my will. The tears fell because I felt hopeless and powerless. I felt like there was nothing I could come up with to change the situation. It was borderline depressing.

Tears falling and all, I knew that I had to finish the job and get the truck out of the way so that the next could pull in. I was well behind the two hours, but I pulled myself together and finished the job. I went to collect my $75. I also let them know that they would not be seeing me again. I was not about to let my life become "that." No more banana trucks. If God wasn't going to open up a door to the NFL, then fine. I could come to terms with that. But I could at least find myself a better job. This wasn't it.

Well, Now What?

Over the next several weeks, anything having to do with football was quiet. No calls. No emails. No football games were even on TV. I refused to spend countless hours searching online for open tryouts. I was back working two jobs again while Levette was back at home taking care of our daughter. We could not afford day care, so she had no choice but to stay home. And I had no choice but to consistently work these boring, monotonous jobs. It was either that or go back to the docks—and anything was better than working the banana truck. So I had more respect for my old jobs when I returned to them this time around.

My jobs may have been less depressing, but I was so far behind in bills due to my inconsistency with bringing money home. The pay from both jobs combined wasn't enough to make up ground on my past due bills and expenses. The only way I could potentially make ends meet was to stop working these two jobs part-time and increase my hours to working full-time at both of jobs. I knew doing this would mean my playing days were over. I just couldn't bring myself to accept that. I chose to stay part time, work hard, but still save at least a small part of my day for football training. I really prayed that

God would see how hard I was trying to do all of this for my family and just give me a break.

The bills steadily outweighed my income. I prayed for a breakthrough. Instead, it just slowly got worse. Finally, it got bad enough that I had to break the lease at our apartment and move out. I could no longer afford the rent. I found us a duplex apartment in a much lower income area of Cleveland. Honestly, this felt like I had reached the lowest of the low. The neighborhood wasn't the safest, and the house wasn't the greatest, but I could afford it with the income I was making. And that meant staying with two part-time jobs was still an option. Which meant so was football.

You might think that I had reverted back to my old college ways again. Maybe football had crept back up to first place again? No. I knew that Christ was first. God was at the top. The Holy Spirit needed to be in the lead. The problem now was simple: I was in love with the sport and I didn't know anything else yet. I knew that only God could open the door. I hadn't quite figured out how to accept the fact that maybe he was saying no. And struggling only made me hungrier. The high salary from pro football could turn my life around in a day. To me, landing an NFL contract was like winning the lottery. I always believed I could do it. And for the sake of my wife, my daughter, my mother, I had to do it.

So no...I wasn't putting football ahead of God. I was just stupidly passionate about making it to the NFL. People needed me, and I saw football as the best thing that I knew how to do to meet those needs. When I finally succeeded, God knew that I was going to give him all the glory. I said that in my prayers all the time, and I meant it with all my heart. For that reason, I thought God was going to help me. Not because I wanted the money but because of my heart.

Déjà vu

Winters in Cleveland are brutal. It's so cold that you use more gas, more electricity, more heat, all of which means more money. I was making just enough to get by, which meant any extra issues would only make things harder on us. It got bad. Now I was having to pick and choose which bills to pay first. Things went from bad to worse when we were late paying our gas bill, and to our surprise, they cut us off. We were in the middle of a Cleveland winter, so I thought for sure that I would have a few days' grace period, and I planned to take care of it. They obviously had no intentions of that.

I thanked God that the electricity was a bill that I could pay in full because it would be a little space heater that kept us warm throughout the first night with no heat. We all went up to the third floor that night, which was the smallest room in the house and the easiest to keep warm. We laid out a bunch of covers, comforters, and quilts to make the carpeted floor a bit softer. That one room became warm enough to where my wife and daughter were able to drift off to sleep. But I never could rest myself. My mind wouldn't allow me. I just stared at the ceiling.

I was lying in a pitch-black room with only the orange-amber glow from the space heater shining and the quiet motor humming. I just started to feel really, really bad. Once again, I had found myself in financial trouble and sitting in the dark with my family. I lay there that night feeling like a failure once again and wondering why this just kept happening to me. I felt like crying, but tears wouldn't even come. I was too frustrated and stressed to let them go. You may be wondering why I didn't just go back to my mother's home. Maybe I should have. But my pride would not let me. I wanted to get my family out of the hole on my own, and most of the night I spent trying to figure out the quickest (and least embarrassing) way to do it.

Chapter 8

THE RESET BUTTON

The next morning was awkward. Nobody was bubbly. We were not arguing or fighting with each other, but we were not happy. My wife looked at me with a clear concern for my state of mind. She knew the night before had hurt my pride. She could clearly see what I was thinking. It was time for change. And not simply a change in jobs or a change in scenery. We needed a change of everything. Attitude. Goals. Methods. Priorities. I knew it, and I knew that Levette felt the same way. But what exactly did that look like? I wasn't quite sure what to do, but I knew better than to keep doing the same thing. I was tired of the insanity, the past due bills, the waiting for NFL teams to call. I was tired of working two low-paying jobs just to make ends meet. I was tired of being tired. Tired of starting over, of failing, of hoping. But I was mostly tired of making the wrong decisions and running into dead ends. Of making too much room for something that wasn't making any room for me.

I knew there had to be a better way to do things. I just needed to figure it out. Levette never stopped believing in me, but her patience with the NFL dream was wearing thin. The morning after our gas got cut off, she looked me square in the eyes and told me the truth. She simply made it clear that this wasn't working and that it was time for change. She made a bunch of great points about how the pursuit of the NFL was not improving our situation but rather making it worse. She reminded me that I needed to drop my pride and understand that it was not about how good I was at playing football but more about my need to face reality.

Levette wanted me to just accept the fact that my plan was not working and to be real with myself but without being so hard on myself. She knew I thought that if I didn't make it to the NFL, anything else was nothing but a failure. But she reminded me that this thinking was wrong, and in fact, the only way that I would become a failure was if I refused to make the right moves when it became crystal clear what those right moves were.

She was right. We had been here before. Too many times, and it was getting old. I knew exactly where she was coming from. Making a living as a pro football player was a dream—not a plan, nor a reality. Then, probably the most powerful thing she said came across as harsh but really was simply a most loving challenge. She told me that *her* father would never allow his family to suffer if he knew there was a way to prevent it. Man, that one stung. *But I was so glad that she said it.* She wanted me to ask myself, *Do we really have to struggle like this?*

No. We didn't.

Her point was made, as clear as day. We didn't *have to* struggle so hard. We were choosing it. I was choosing it for us. There are some people who literally cannot go out and work jobs, having no choice but to struggle. But I *could* do something about my plight if I could just get over the fact that maybe my options would not include playing football.

So I made up my mind that I was willing to do anything that it would take to make life better for all of us. Literally anything. I would even have gone back to the bananas if I had too. Probably. (Maybe.) But that was neither here nor there (thank God) because that job didn't fit the new plan. Little weird or temporary odd job days were done. It was time to find a solid situation that checked all the boxes according to our needs.

We prayed for guidance, and we landed on a plan. We decided I would go back to school and finish my degree. This was the most sensible thing to do. But we hadn't the slightest idea how to make it happen.

I picked up the phone, and I called the University of Louisville. They had a program that allowed former athletes to come back and finish their degrees, free of charge. It was basically a continuation of my scholarship, picking right up where I left off. I asked if I was in good enough standing to enroll in the program. I was, and I did. The next week, we spent every day preparing to make the trek back to Louisville. My priorities were in place, and my goals were as follows: find a job, find an apartment, and finish school.

I made a few more calls to a few key places ahead of my return to Louisville. One of them was to my former arena football team to ask if I could return. My agreement with Levette was that if football ever became a part of the plan, then it had to make sense—through prayer and practicality. It did, with both. I made a few hundred dollars a week consisting of a minimal time commitment to the football team, and all the rest of the time was spent working at a GNC store making decent, dependable money. And, if I were to get hurt and couldn't play football, GNC was still a job that I could show up and do. We had a plan.

So playing arena football and working at a local GNC while finishing up my degree became my new way of life. I was working hard every day and bringing home a paycheck every two weeks. I paid my bills on time, nothing was being cut off, and I was taking care of my family. Then on the weekends, I was able to play the sport that I loved in front of the fans that I loved. I felt blessed. Content for the moment. I was scratching my pro football itch while getting paid a little extra money to do it. And several weeks later I found myself just a few college credits away from completing the necessary requirements to claim my Bachelor of Science degree from the University of Louisville. One final class, one last assignment and later that year, May 8, 2004, I became the first person in my family to graduate college.

The Acting Bug Resurfaces—and Bites

After I graduated college in May of 2004, my life took an unexpected turn. I just so happened to be watching the Animal Planet channel, and I saw that they were holding auditions for a reality television show called *King of the Jungle*.

The premise of the show was for twelve contestants to come together from all across the country to compete in a series of tests and challenges for the opportunity to host their own nature show on Animal Planet. Now this actually happened to be the second season for the show, and we thoroughly enjoyed watching season one.

I considered auditioning for the show and asked Levette what she thought about it. We prayed about it and felt led to give it a shot. Immediately, we began to go to work on creating an audition tape to submit. With thousands of people submitting auditions, we knew that we needed to do something special—something that would pop and separate me from the rest of the pack.

Back when I was in college at Louisville, I worked during the summers at the Louisville Zoo. The zoo gladly pulled a few strings for us, allowing me to use some of the exhibits to make my audition tape. I had the lions roaring right on cue, goats giving me a "high five," and I even managed to fit a few football highlights in there in any way I could. My tape had just about everything, so it definitely stood out. We submitted the video to Animal Planet and then simply went on with life. Making the audition tape was a lot of fun, and we all were pretty excited, but none of us really expected the network to select me.

But sure enough, just a few weeks later, I got the call from Animal Planet that I was an official selection for season two of *King of the Jungle*. I could not believe it! What are the odds? Thousands of applicants, only twelve were selected, and I made the cut. If that wasn't unbelievable enough, not only did I make the cut, but I also *won* the whole thing! It was so crazy. If you've never seen this show, just think *Survivor* but with animals involved in all the challenges. It was a game of wits, strength, power, and animal knowledge. And after twelve weeks of competition, I was crowned season two's "King of the Jungle." It was an unbelievable time. Getting selected to be on the show was already cool enough, but to win the whole thing was just amazing.

The reward for winning *King of the Jungle* was a decent cash prize and an all-expense paid trip to Australia to film my own one-hour television special with Animal Planet. I couldn't believe all of this was really happening. It felt so good for things to start going my way again, for a situation to be in my favor and occurring in a pleasing, successful way, rather than some form of disappointment. I truly felt like I had hit the reset button on my life.

After I was finished with all the filming, it was time to truly enjoy the best part of it all—watching everything being released on television. Of course, with reality TV, we are contractually obligated to not tell anyone the results of the show. So for ten weeks, we were all watching each episode one by one, and only Levette knew that I was the winner. Each week, as the number of contestants dwindled down to the final four, the city of Louisville was rooting for me to win. That's when the news coverage started, and the reporters were saying, "Well, it looks like Stallings has survived another week" and the like. I was still playing football for the Louisville Fire (my arena team), and many of them would hold watch parties for the show at local restaurants. Soon everyone would see me win the entire competition, and then a week later, we would all watch my Animal Planet one-hour special, for which I was the host. I'll never forget when the local news showed up to my apartment, and I went to several stations for a few live interviews. I know I'm originally from Cleveland, but that day I truly felt like one of Louisville's own.

After everything died down, I had the opportunity to reflect on the whole TV experience. Two and a half months I had been on TV every Tuesday night. I started to feel as though I could really get used to that. Now reality TV wasn't really my thing, and I didn't really enjoy the drama. But when I went to Australia to film my own show, well, that was completely different. As the host of my own show, I was able to experience what a true production schedule felt like. Everything was scripted and well planned out. As the host, I had to attend production meetings and blocking practice (rehearsing the different places where I would be standing or moving while filming), rehearsals, and other kinds of run throughs. I had lines to learn and scenes to act out. I very much enjoyed this environment. I loved everything about it and could easily see myself making a living doing something similar. When it was all over, I missed it.

It became obvious to both me and my wife that the acting bug had taken a nice big chunk out of me. So although football remained my number one love, acting in film and television pulled up in a close and unexpected second place. And if I'm really honest, I'd say that it was almost dead even. But I still felt like I had something to prove on the football field. I still felt that I had what it took to make it to the NFL.

And although my chasing of the NFL became a bit tamer, I didn't lose any confidence. In fact, I gained even more. Almost weekly, I was seeing players get called up from the arena league to much higher-level leagues, including the NFL.

All I needed to do was keep shining on the field each week when I played. For the Louisville Fire, I had begun to break records and claim several "player of the week" honors. So after my television stint had ended, I returned to the arena league and continued to dominate. To celebrate my national television win, I made an entrance with a twelve-foot Burmese python draped across my shoulders! The announcer said, "And straight from the jungle, now back to the field...the *King of the Jungle!*" Then I appeared with my snake, slowly, surrounded by plumes of smoke. I went on to have a great game that night.

I was really enjoying everything about everything. That's the best way to describe it. I was happy. My family was happy. My faith was in good shape. My finances were solid. My football dream was still very much alive, and now, I had a much more responsible way of chasing it. Acting was a new passion, something I had begun to wonder if I potentially had a future with. But acting was something that I could do my whole life. The same with working a nine to five. As I got older, the football window was closing, and I hadn't quite given up on the NFL just yet.

Chapter 9

ONE LAST TIME

Life after being on TV for most of the fall in 2004 was nice. My brief reality TV stardom quickly spilled over into the Louisville community. I had begun to do animal education shows at various schools around the city. After *King of the Jungle*, my personal reptile and exotic pet collection had grown tremendously, and I also partnered with a local pet store to bring in huge snakes, baby gators, tarantulas, larger lizards, and other exotic animals that I didn't already own to showcase at the schools. The kids always loved this, for they got a chance to see up close many animals that they probably would never otherwise see in person. When the 2005 arena football season started, the Louisville Fire football team continued to allow me to use my twelve-foot reticulated python as a prop during player introductions. The fans loved it, and I was having such a good time.

At this point of my life, it was nice to see people enjoying me perform both on the football field and on television. But reality TV stardom quickly comes and goes. Once again, even stronger this time, I fantasized about being an actor. I began to wonder what it might be like to be a full-time actor one day, rather than a one-time reality TV star. I tucked that thought away in the back of my mind for safekeeping. Then I would go on the arena football field and put on a show.

My talent on the arena football field soon got the attention of the CFL's Calgary Stampeders. They contacted my agent and invited me up to Canada for an invite-only workout. My agent cautioned me to take this workout with a grain of salt because there would be about a hundred or so other athletes invited, but the opportunity was, in fact, a legit one. He also let me know that the team would not be covering my flight. This meant that I had to use my own money if I wanted to attend this tryout. That's when the details about this tryout opportunity started to concern me.

I absolutely wanted to go, but the price of a plane ticket would put a dent in my finances. At that time, I wasn't way ahead financially, but I wasn't behind either. I was in a decent place, and I was being responsible with my family's money. It wouldn't take much to mess things up and put us in the dark again, as I had already done twice before. But I would be lying if I didn't tell you that everything in me was burning with a desire to go to this tryout in Canada. I was making $200 a week playing for the Fire, barely $3,000 for the entire season. If I were to make a roster for the Stampeders, I could make twenty times that much. This was my first truly legit life-changing pro football opportunity. It would also put me much closer to the NFL because I would be back playing outdoors. I had no idea what to do.

When I discussed this opportunity with my wife and we prayed about all the details, we decided to boldly take the opportunity. At this stage of our marriage and our life, we had become very diligent about praying through everything. My wife was the type of woman (and still is today) who does not mind getting behind me if she knows that I'm following Jesus. We both knew that everything God leads us to does not come with a guarantee that it will be easy. It doesn't always make sense in the beginning. But our commitment to each other, after so many missteps, was that we'd do everything to make sure that all our choices were always God-led. We knew the only way to be sure of that was through consistent prayer. So, we did just that.

Our prayer life gave us the confidence to sacrifice the money needed to fly up to Canada for the tryout. With Levette being on board, I just needed to take advantage of this opportunity and make the sacrifice count. I began to do everything that I could to set myself up to succeed. This meant making the tough decision about whether I should play in my next arena football game or not. The CFL tryout was just two days after my upcoming arena football game. An injury playing for the Fire would almost certainly erase my CFL opportunity. But since I had gotten this information from my agent so close to my next arena game, there was no time to replace me in the lineup. I felt as though abandoning my team at the last minute like this would not go over well with the coaches or my teammates. And since there were no guarantees that I would make the team up in Canada, it would be stupid to burn the bridge with the Louisville Fire. So I decided to play in the game that weekend.

And of course, *I got hurt.*

Decisions, Decisions

I had severely sprained my ankle in the game so much that I could not put pressure on my foot. I was devastated. I had already booked my flight for Calgary, my excitement had been through the roof, and now here I was with a fat ankle. I remember telling Levette that it appeared my ankle made the decision for me. She felt so bad for me. We just prayed together, decided to go to bed, and reassess things in the morning. When we got up the next day, I stepped out of the bed, and my ankle was very stiff and painful. Throughout the day I did some rehab on my ankle, attempting to loosen it up a bit. The improvement was minimal, but at least I could walk, and it wasn't as swollen. But running seemed to be out of the question. Making sharp cuts and playing fast would be the only way to be impressive, and I didn't think that I would be able to. I only had a day and a half before I'd need to be able to perform.

It only made sense to cancel my flight to Canada rather than waste $500 on the plane tickets. I felt that this would be the responsible thing to do. So you can imagine my shock when Levette suggested that I actually stay committed to going up to Canada for the tryout. She reminded me that we had been in prayer and that we believed that God had opened the door for me to go. I felt the same way, but I thought it was just me. Knowing that we were joined in our thinking and praying and that we agreed it was right for me to coura-geously go and just figure it out when I got there, I felt a ton of air beneath my wings. My bad ankle and I hobbled onto a plane and headed to Canada to give everything we had to the Calgary Stampeders—that is if my ankle would cooperate.

When I arrived in Calgary, I spent the whole day working on my ankle. I used every rehabilitation technique that I had learned throughout my life. Walking and bending, raising up on my toes, and rotating my foot became easier and easier to do throughout the day. I had worked my ankle so much that by the end of that night, it felt exponentially better. Although it was still painful, I was actually rather optimistic. I honestly did not think that I would get a chance to show what I could do on the field. The whole point of flying up to Canada on a bad ankle was to at least meet the coaches and maybe sit down with them and watch my highlights. I hoped to be able to tell them that my season in the arena league was going tremendously well and assure them that I would heal up and get right back to dominating. I figured I could at least accomplish that much if my ankle failed me. But this rehab was going much better than I expected, and maybe—with a decent enough tape job on my ankle—there was a small chance that I could actually do some running around at the tryout. How the ankle felt the next morning would tell me all I needed to know.

More Decisions, Decisions

When I woke up in the morning, I was extremely optimistic. Lying in the bed, my ankle felt pretty good. As soon as I put my foot to the floor and stood on it, my optimism tanked. I could barely walk again. It felt so stiff, almost as bad as it felt when I first injured it. Now I was starting to feel like I might have worked it too hard, too much, for too long during rehab.

I had to figure out exactly what I was going to do. I needed a plan. I did not want to take the field on a bad ankle and look horrible because that wouldn't be a true representation of my skills. At the same time, I didn't think the coaches would be extremely interested in players who came to talk versus players who came to play. I wasn't quite sure what route to take.

When I arrived at the Calgary Stampeders training facility, I refused to limp or give any hint that I was hurting. Until I knew in my mind what I was going to do, there would be no talk of a sprained ankle. I decided to head to the training room and begin warming up and rehabbing my ankle. I began to notice that the warm water, the stretching, and just the working of the muscles in and around the ankle started to loosen everything up. I kept this up until I could get it to feel as good as possible. Immediately, I got dressed and had the trainers tape both of my ankles. I would decide whether to play or to just meet with the coaches once I hopped off the training table and put my feet to the floor.

When I landed, my ankle felt amazing. It was almost back to normal, and I couldn't believe it. I was pretty sure what was happening. My ankle was warm, the muscles were primed from the treatment, and the tape job was effectively supporting the weaker ligaments. And while I can't prove it, I believe I had a bit of healing from the Lord. And even if he, in fact, did not supernaturally make my pain go away, I can for sure say that he led me down the right path of rehab that would allow me to perform as pain free as possible. I wasn't 100 percent, but whatever percent the Lord allowed me to have that day was more than enough because I tore up that tryout.

A few days later while working at GNC, my agent called and told me that the coaches felt my performance was excellent. They did not say that they were going to sign me, but I still took this as good news. It validated my trip. And even if I did not get signed to a contract, I appreciated the way my faith had grown throughout this process. If nothing else came of this tryout, I knew for sure that I had grown spiritually. This was the topic of discussion that night with my wife. Levette was so proud of me.

While we were seated on the floor in the living room, my cellphone rang. It was my agent. He informed me to not make plans for the upcoming summer because I would be spending it as a Calgary Stampeder! When I tell you that the smile on my face could have lit up the whole city, even *that* might be an understatement. My wife and I laughed, we cried, then we celebrated, then we picked up the phone to call friends and family, then we prayed together and thanked God over and over again. I had finally done it. I was officially a big-time professional football player. It wasn't the NFL, but this was the closest thing to it. It was so satisfying to me because even if I never got any higher, the CFL could meet all my needs—financially and athletically. A long career in the CFL was nothing to sneeze at, and I would always be on the doorstep of the NFL. All I had to do was keep playing well and let the rest take care of itself. That's exactly what I did.

After spending much of my rookie season on the bench, I finally got activated for the playoffs. On my very first play, I ran for an electrifying sixty-three yards and nearly scored. I went on to have a great game, receiving co-player of the game (sharing the honor with our quarterback) for my outstanding performance, making a name for myself in the only game I ever started at running back for the Stampeders in 2005. This showing in the playoffs gained me a three-year extension with the team. Optimism for next year was high, and I had found my football home.

"Happy" Anniversary

The 2006 Calgary Stampeders season had begun four weeks prior to my five-year wedding anniversary. My wife and I still lived in Louisville, so they could not come up to Canada to be with me during training camp. I had planned to surprise my wife by asking her not to renew our lease in Louisville and to come to Canada to be with me throughout the entire season instead. After four weeks of training camp, no injuries, and a pretty good showing, the prerequisites that I had were complete, and I felt comfortable going through with my plan. So Levette gave up our little apartment, and I flew her up to Calgary in the wee hours of the night on June 8, 2006.

When I picked her and my daughter up from the airport, they were surprised to see that I was no longer in the team provided housing, but I had gotten us our own apartment. We had our own bedroom, and our daughter had hers. I had everything furnished and ready. This was my anniversary gift to Levette. We didn't even go to sleep but stayed up until sunrise. That morning marked are fifth year anniversary. I told her that I loved her so much and would not be on this team if not for her supporting me, and I did not want her to miss a moment.

That same morning, I had a pretty good practice on the field. Many players knew that I had flown my family up to be with me on my anniversary and were wishing me well. At about noon, we had a team meeting. Right after this meeting, the head coach called me into his office. Thirty minutes later I walked out of that meeting no longer a Calgary Stampeder. They had cut me. This was shocking on so many levels. There were absolutely no signs pointing towards me being released. I had just been featured in Calgary's newspaper a couple of days prior, and I played well in the preseason games. I certainly would not have flown my wife up to be with me if I had any idea that I was going to be cut. I couldn't believe it.

But this is when I learned for the first time how harsh the business of pro football could be. Because it turns out that they had no plans to cut me until a player that they had been pursuing from the NFL became available at the very last minute. I was aware that things didn't add up when a fourth running back joined our usual staple of three. I knew someone was going to be cut. But I outplayed this other person in the preseason, so I didn't think it would be me. But I was wrong. I suppose having that NFL tag next to his name held a lot of weight.

I was not the only one surprised by the cut. My teammates did not believe that Calgary had released me until they saw me grab a large black trash bag and began stuffing my belongings into it. When it became obvious that this was not a joke, the players began to console me with lots of hugs and plenty of sad faces. A bittersweet part of this situation was the outpouring of support from non-players. The desk assistant was crying. Other administrative people were sad for me. And this let me know that I had done more at Calgary than just come in and out as a football player. I had formed meaningful relationships and carried myself in a way that Jesus would be proud of. Although I was hurting and extremely disappointed—downright angry—it was the reality of my impact that gave me some sense of dignity and peace. I did not want to let my anger mess any of this up on my way out, and I decided to put Jesus ahead of my personal feelings. I wanted the last impression I gave to the team, the organization, Stampeder fans, and CFL fans nationwide to be one that says *God is still good.* And that's exactly what I did.

After I finished shaking hands, hugging, and saying goodbyes, I exited the back of the facility. I was still a bit shocked, even as reality set in while I carried the large trash bag filled with my stuff. And the moment I turned the corner, coming out into the open from behind the Stampeder facility, I was bombarded by several news reporters waiting for me outside of the complex. Apparently, all of them were just as shocked to see me cut. They were asking me to make a statement. They all felt that I had been done wrong and highlighted how unfair the move was. The more they highlighted the ruthlessness of the cut, the more my anger began to rebuild. So I said a quick prayer and reminded myself to give God glory on the way out. I took a few moments to do just that, but then sadness came over me when I remembered that Levette didn't know that any of this had happened. Happy anniversary.

When I got back to the apartment, the TV was on one of Canada's sports stations. Levette seemed to be having a good time putting things away and organizing Christian's new room. I broke the news to her, and it broke her heart. Her pain was a little bit different than mine because most of it was due to seeing me hurt. She was so tired of football not giving back to me what I was giving to it. Moments later, we could see on the TV that it had been announced that I had been surprisingly cut. Later, an article would surface with the title: "Happy Anniversary, Tony Gets the Boot." (You can still read this news article online today.) We were all extremely disappointed and sad. We loaded up our car and proceeded to make the thirty-three-hour drive back to Louisville, Kentucky. Levette wasn't the only one getting tired of my heart being crushed by football. I wasn't sure if I could take another blow like this one. It was not exactly the way I planned to spend my anniversary.

Bergamo

After returning to the States, I quickly jumped on another arena team for 2007, but it felt like a huge step back. So I refused to play arena football again. At this point I was about to turn thirty and had begun to consider life after football. Whether I liked it or not, I knew that retirement was fast approaching, and a transition plan needed to be in place. My wife and I prayed about such a plan and felt led to commit to playing football for only one more year.

The year 2008 became all about finding one last, respectable, legit playing opportunity that could also fund the family as well. Those were the stipulations. We were dead set on meeting these requirements, and if we could not do so, then we agreed to seek God's wisdom for a career path that did not have anything to do with playing pro football.

This meant putting on a suit and tie, grabbing my degree, and putting it to work. Or maybe it meant continuing in ministry at a church. I didn't know exactly what the next stage would be, but I knew it was something that I needed to start thinking more about.

It was during this time that I received an email from a professional football team overseas—in Bergamo, Italy. A friend of mine from the Calgary Stampeders was a friend of the head coach for the Bergamo Lions, a professional American football team in Europe. Bergamo was badly in need of a good running back, and my friend told him that I had just been cut and would be a perfect fit. After talking with the head coach and discussing what my pay would be, it met all the requirements that Levette and I had discussed.

I should also mention that Levette had become pregnant for a second time. She was early in the term, and if she were to come to Bergamo with me, we could run the risk of not being able to return and have our child in the States. The idea of being away from our trusted doctors and caretakers for this pregnancy did not sit well with either of us. I considered turning the Bergamo Lions down. But Levette looked at me and said, "One more time, sweetheart." She was giving me her blessing to go on without her. Part of this was because we needed the money, but most of it was because she wanted me to get it all out of my system. She wanted me to finish well and to do so at a high level. We saw that many former professional athletes from both the NFL and the CFL were participants in this league. We agreed that once this season was over, I would retire if it didn't do something impressive enough to lead me to the NFL or back to the CFL. This was my last shot. *One more time.*

And in 2008, I had the season of my life as a professional. For the Bergamo Lions, I gained over fifteen hundred yards, made twenty-six touchdowns, and was the team's most valuable player. A very special moment for me happened halfway through the season when my wife called and told me that we were having a baby boy! I announced it to all my Italian teammates, and they went crazy. Everybody was yelling and congratulating me. My father-in-law (*God rest his soul*) was with my wife, and he yelled into the phone, "Tell that ole Egg Noggin' to score four touchdowns for me!" (Yep, his nickname for me was "Egg Noggin'.")

He told me to get him four, and I did him one better. The next day I scored five touchdowns in a big win over Spain and was named the game's most valuable player. It's fair to say that I was excited about the good news concerning my new son and had no problem putting all of that energy to good use. But I missed my wife and daughter, my mother, and my in-laws. I looked forward to getting back to America. Nonetheless, I was having the time of my life in Europe. The only thing that would have made it better is if my wife and daughter were with me. I saw more countries in one season than most people see in a lifetime. Most importantly, I was tearing it up on the field. I would eventually lead my team to the championship game, and we won it all. (They actually call it the Super Bowl too!) Doing so well against respectable competition increased my hopes of getting either the CFL or NFL's attention. I could not wait to get back to the States, put together a highlight reel, and let my agent get to work. Certainly, if I had been able to get the attention of Calgary Stampeders based on my success in the arena league, *surely* winning a Super Bowl in Europe and putting up some seriously impressive stats should make some headlines.

Sidenote, I need to say this. I remain to this day most grateful to the Bergamo Lions football organization and my Calgary teammate who made the connection for me. Professionally, this was the most rewarding season, emotionally and statistically, that I ever had in my career as a player. Now it was time to go home and capitalize.

A Sudden Loss

In the months leading up to me returning home from Europe, my father-in-law fell ill and was hospitalized. His encouragement for me to have a good game were the last words I personally heard him say. He eventually took a turn for the worse and slipped into a coma for several weeks. I returned home to see him during the coma. It was tough to go back and forth to the hospital with Levette. Walking away each night after visiting hours came to an end was always tough on her. You will never understand how hard unless you knew both my wife and her dad. These two were inseparable. I'll never forget being at the hospital with the both of them. Her dad was incoherent yet still seemed to be somewhat aware of her presence. She'd be holding his large hands and just talking to him, hoping he would speak back. He never would. It's almost as though he was *there,* but *not there* at the same time. She always hoped that he would pull through, and she never gave up on that hope. But soon, my wife would lose her dad to complications from pneumonia.

Knowing the type of man that Levette's father was, the type of example he was, the type of hard-working provider he was, truly motivated me to protect her with my own life—just as he always did. I know for a fact he cared about Levette very much and had entrusted me to do the same ever since giving me his blessing on our wedding day. The last thing I wanted to do was fail at honoring that standard. So I refused to let him down. I would make it my goal to honor his life by always treating his daughter the way he would have wanted her to be treated. With the same kind of love that he gave her: unconditional, unbreakable, and inseparable.

In Memory of "Big Joe" Robinson

Rest in Christ.

Chapter 10

A CHANGE OF PASSION

After having such a good season for the Bergamo Lions, I was certain that the CFL or NFL teams would come calling. My agent had begun to see what he could do with my impressive showing overseas, but no teams were biting on it. In my mind, it was still early in the process, and I was willing to stay patient. There were plenty of other things to focus on while my agent worked on my behalf. I had already failed enough times due to putting all my eggs in one basket and becoming stagnant, so I refused to go back down that path. I began to finally pray about a plan B, in case I had truly just played my final pro football game. It was odd; the whole "plan B" thing. I had to really think about something that I hadn't ever given much thought to: *What exactly did I think I wanted to do with my life if football did not pan out?*

I loved doing ministry, so I began to volunteer as a teacher for my local church. Being involved with Fellowship of Christian Athletes also provided volunteer teaching opportunities to the youth. I loved coaching football, so I took a small job doing that as well. Slowly but surely, I was understanding how to prioritize my personal *and* my professional lives. I was starting not only to put things in the proper order but also to listen to wise counsel on ways to keep them that way. These were just a few of the building blocks necessary for the level of maturity that I would need soon. God was preparing the soil. I believe he was slowly transforming my outlook on life so that I could allow him to lead me in making some key decisions for my family down the road.

The Set Up

One Sunday I noticed that some members of our church were having auditions for a new acting ministry called "KidWay." KidWay presentations would occur once a month on Sundays and would feature stage plays that taught students biblical life lessons and principles. This was a new ministry at the church, and the cast members had yet to be selected. I thought that this was a very clever ministry idea and decided to audition. I landed a starring role in the cast, and we began rehearsing for the first show a few weeks later. We would spend a few weeks learning the skits, and then we would put on the performance at the end of each month. I became good friends with the cast, and I absolutely loved putting on the performances.

Probably one of the most fun activities that took my mind off the anxiety of waiting for the NFL or CFL to call was participating in this acting ministry and teaching the kids about Jesus. On the other hand, I sometimes think that this was just Jesus setting me up. You remember that acting bug that bit me back in my *King of the Jungle*/Animal Planet days? And you remember how I said I pretty much put acting in the back of my mind? Well that bug took a second bite, and the desire to perform as an actor slowly began to creep from the back towards the front. Most of what I'm saying now is hindsight. Back when all of this was happening, I loved KidWay as just a very cool and purposeful way to pass time. But I think God was using this acting ministry to plant a seed that he would later allow to grow and bloom.

Fireproof

One day after a routine rehearsal for the next KidWay show, one of the cast members invited my wife and me to go see a movie called *Fireproof.* I was unfamiliar with the film and asked for a few details. When I was told that it was a movie about marriage, I wasn't that excited about it. But I loved hanging out with the cast, and we would often do things together, so Levette and I agreed to go. We were late getting to the theater, so we had to sit in the very front seats. I always wondered who would ever choose those seats. You have to look almost straight up at the ceiling to watch the film!

Maybe sitting in the very front row was where I was meant to be because I was able to see a very compelling sight. By the time the movie ended, the whole room had been impacted. As I looked up at the screen and the credits were rolling, I could hear so many people crying. I turned around and could see that these were tears of joy. Some were tears of thankfulness because the film led to several men asking for forgiveness from their wives, and the wives were extending that forgiveness. Men and women sat in that theater and were reconciling with each other in their marriages. That was a powerful thing to see. And they were not alone because I was one of them.

I had been married for seven years and thought that I was doing a pretty good job. But this movie raised the standard for me. I knew I could be better. Levette and my family needed to get my best. And it had blown me away that this revelation came from a simple film about doing marriage God's way. After promising Levette that I would be fully committed to becoming the husband that God had called me to be, I then experienced a burning passion in my heart. I wanted to become an actor. Just like that, right then and there, I knew I wanted to act. And I knew that I didn't want to be just any actor. I did not want to run to Hollywood and try to become famous and be willing to just take any role that was thrown my way. No, I wanted to do films that honored God. I wanted to be a part of a production that made people feel the way I and the others in that theater were feeling.

My heart began to beat with force. My excitement was through the roof. The only other time I would feel this way was when football was involved. But this time, for the first time, this fire and passion had nothing to do with football but had everything to do with becoming an actor that God could use for his glory. I couldn't believe what was happening, but I knew what I now wanted to do with my life. Right there in that movie theater, while I was watching *Fireproof* in 2008, God had shifted my passions to acting. Playing football took a back seat, and a whole new set of desires took its place. After gathering my thoughts, I turned to Levette and shared with her what I was feeling. I told her that we needed to start praying about this together, immediately, because I needed clarity from God. I needed to know if I was just being a prisoner of the moment or if this was really him putting this desire in my heart.

We saw that the "Kendrick Brothers and Sherwood Pictures" were responsible for making *Fireproof*. So I knew what I had to do. That night when Levette and I got home, I told her that we needed to immediately start praying about working with the Kendrick Brothers. That night, I gave my plan to the Lord. I begged him to validate what was in my heart. If he was behind this new passion, we asked him to make it abundantly clear. If this desire to become a professional actor was not of him, we then asked that he shut down that desire altogether. After prayer, I went to bed peacefully—yet extremely excited about how God would answer.

Cable Guy

Until I received validation with acting, I still held on to hope of making an NFL team in my back pocket. And one thing I had learned over time was that in order to keep Levette on board with my NFL pursuits, there could be no more financial struggles. So I always kept an eye out for a way to add even the slightest bit of revenue. The only problem was the limitations that I always placed on the type of job opportunity I was willing to take. In one way or another, my freedom to try out for football teams remained a big part of the criteria. Sometimes bigger than I realized. I tried to find something that would give me the flexibility to train for football yet provide some form of steady income. This led to me doing door-to-door sales. Commission based, door-to-door sales. For a cable company. I was hesitant to do this because I hated sales. But they were hiring like crazy, and it checked all the boxes for the situation I was in. The hiring process was quick. I could create my own hours. There was no limit to how much I could potentially make.

At first, I was worried about someone recognizing me and ridiculing me for working a door-to-door sales job. Good thing it was the winter. I wore a big coat and a thick winter skull cap pulled low, so I was somewhat incognito. The job was simple. I walk up onto your porch, knock at your door, make my pitch, you take it or leave it, and then I'm out of there. Not too bad. In the beginning, it was okay. I made a few sales, and nobody was hovering over me. Except one day in particular was so traumatizing for me that it would be my last day on this job. I'll never forget it.

It was a cold night, and I was hitting my last couple of houses for the day. This day had not been so good. In fact, the last few weeks had not been so good. Lots of noes. Of course, that meant trouble with finances at home. Nothing was happening with football either. My mood wasn't that great. But I had to put on a smile and try to make a sale. I approached a well-lit porch and rang the doorbell. A woman came to the door, and like always, I gave my pitch. She seemed extremely intrigued and decided to go talk to her husband for a moment. She closed the door halfway. Moments later, a little boy came to the door and said hi. He was probably ten or eleven maybe. After I responded, he looked at me again, then ran off. *That was weird*, I thought. Then he came back with his mom and dad. In his hand, he had one of my University of Louisville game worn gloves. I had signed it for him after one of my college games. The mother said, "Are you Tony Stallings—the star player for the Louisville Fire?"

Shocked that the little boy had recognized me so easily, I nodded. I was completely caught off guard, and now I was becoming slightly embarrassed. I kept my composure though. Then the mother said, "Oh my goodness! My son recognized you right away! He has your football glove—you signed it for him, and let me tell you—you were one of his favorite players!" I was smiling at this point, of course. It wasn't so bad hearing from a young fan like this. Then her son stepped in front of her with the signed glove and said, "What are you doing out here selling cable?"

Good feeling *gone*.

All my confidence left me. I wanted to disappear. Man, I felt so bad and stupid. I was completely embarrassed. I didn't even know how to answer. I told him that I just hadn't made it to the NFL yet, but I'm going to keep trying. I couldn't wait to get out of there. I don't even remember if I completed the sale or not. I *do* remember feeling unbelievably bad though. Looking at that kid's face made me feel like I had let him down. He was old enough to know that really good players go on to the NFL after college, not onto his porch with cable brochures. *I was a good player, little boy. I* still *am,* I kept thinking. *I just don't know how to explain to you why you're watching me sell cable on your porch instead of scoring touchdowns on your TV.*

This was an ego blow like no other.

The walk back to my car felt long—like they were still staring at me from their front porch. I didn't look back. It was cold and dark, and my pride was under my feet. Then, while I'm already feeling worthless, it started to rain. *Hard.* It was pouring now, and I had parked pretty far down the street near my first house stop. I ran for my car and quickly got in, started the engine, cranked up the heat, and just sat there for a minute. I stared back at that last house for a moment. Then I called Levette. I told her what happened, and that sales were not for me. She knew this little boy had hurt my pride. This stung. She didn't get mad about me quitting the job. She wasn't comfortable with me losing a source of income, but she didn't go in on me about that. Levette mostly displayed measured calmness and understanding. But I knew what she was thinking. She knew what I was thinking.

I'm better than this.

I Heard God Loud and Clear

My heart still possessed a desire to play professionally—if the Lord would allow. I decided to see if there was a local professional team that I could play on. The Louisville Fire would have been the obvious choice, but financial problems had led to them ceasing operations. Shut door number one. I ended up finding another arena league team to play on, but after a few practices, that team lost its funding as well, and it ceased operations. Shut door number two.

Still keeping a humble attitude, I found yet another team to play for locally, this time, even lower than the arena level. This was semi-pro football. You don't even get paid to play. I was far too talented for something like this, but in my view, it was just a way to stay sharp and have fun. It was local and light duty. I would still have guys trying to catch me and tackle me, regardless of the talent level. This was just a way to keep the juices flowing—like I said—basically a glorified training session. Whatever my reasons were for agreeing to play in this uninsured, non-paying, outdoor, full contact football league did not matter to my wife. She did *not* want me to do it. Levette hated the idea. And for good reason. Honestly, it was a very *bad* idea for me. But maybe it was just what I needed to do in order to move forward in life.

The first semi-pro football game day had arrived. As I said, this was full contact, outdoor, NFL-style football. We were all padded up, helmets and shoulder pads and everything else. We had a decent sized crowd, PA announcers, real referees, and even cheerleaders. The league was legit, but it was definitely not for me. No pay, no insurance, and really nothing to gain. Levette warned me not to play. But I shrugged it off. What's the worst that could happen?

The game started, and I was tearing it up. After a couple touchdowns and running all over the opposing team, things seemed to be going as planned. But a few plays later, a really heavy guy tackled me and in such a way that caused a very sharp pain in my chest. It felt like something from my shoulder pads was poking me. It wasn't a pain that I had ever felt before, and I had experienced my fair share of injuries over the years. I stayed in the game and ran another play. This time, I was tackled much softer. The guy barely touched me, but it now hurt my chest just to run. As I walked back to the huddle for the next play, the pain *really* intensified, so I U-turned and came out of the game. The trainer took off my shoulder pads, ran his fingers across my chest, and told me that two of my ribs were broken.

I had never broken a rib before, so it didn't completely dawn on me right away what that meant in terms of seriousness. As the trainer continued to check my ribs and as the time passed, all the adrenaline that I had left was replaced by *pain*. Excruciating pain. After about three minutes, the pain was radiating through my whole upper body. It felt like someone was trying to pull my chest apart with pliers. Now every move I made caused unbearable pain. Breathing hurt. Walking hurt. Sitting hurt. Standing hurt. Everything hurt.

Levette came rushing down in a panic, and her demeanor got worse when they told her my ribs were dislocated and cracked. Now it was time to get me to the hospital, and with no team insurance, we were on our own to cover this expense. The nearest hospital was downtown, and adding insult to injury, this happened to be the same hospital in which her father died. She was certain to have a PTSD-type of experience.

The car ride to the hospital was the most painful part of the situation. I felt every bump. Fear started to set in that I might have punctured a lung. I felt terrible putting Levette and my children through this. Thoughts of never touching another football again entered my head. The pain was unrelenting. Other than the dislocation of my elbow, I had never known an injury in which the pain just kept growing and growing rather than simmering down over time. Then it got even worse when we arrived at the emergency room because we had to wait in line. So I sat in the waiting room, writhing in agony, for what felt like an eternity. Finally, my name was called. I could barely get up. I was wheeled away to a room and placed in a hospital bed. The rest of the night I do not remember. I was sedated while they reset my ribs.

That whole ordeal was bad enough, but what made it worse was the impact it had on Levette and the kids. They were not allowed to be in the hospital room. She had to walk away from me the same way she walked away from her dad, in that exact same hospital. I hated to have put her though all the anxiety, stress, and fear. Once again, the thoughts of retiring from any kind of professional football activity ran through my mind. I began to think that this was clearly a locking, shutting, and bolting of the football door. That's why I say that maybe it was a good thing that it happened. God seemed to have been shutting doors before I joined this league, sending the message of *no* in a much less painful way. But if that was indeed the message he was trying to send, I can tell you that I honestly missed it unintentionally. Maybe he decided to deliver the message in such a way that it couldn't be missed. If so, he succeeded.

Eventually I would endure a rough, painful healing process. But I did heal. Even to this day, remnants of my calcified ribs protrude ever so slightly. In my mind, after the rehab and healing, I had pretty much come to the conclusion that God was telling me that the chase needed to end. That made the most sense. No NFL team ever called. No league of *any kind* called. And when someone is coming off the extraordinary season that I had in Europe, it simply didn't make sense for no offers to come in. Except, I suppose, it did make sense. God was saying *no*.

Perspective truly is everything. I needed to choose the right one, even if it was unfavorable in my eyes. God emphatically shut the door. And this time, I think he meant business. And as bad as it was, that punctured lung scare had the potential to be so much worse. I was told by doctors that the best thing about my injury was that the ribs broke outward, not inward (towards any vital organs). Sometimes that can be fatal. I heard the Lord loud and clear. I believed that he was putting a nail in the coffin of my football plans completely. I officially had no problem with it. This last ordeal was enough for me to become at least 99 percent sure that I would no longer play pro football. Why leave the 1 percent? Well, you just never say *never*, even though I was pretty sure that it was time to retire. Nonetheless, I might as well have been 100 percent sure. That rib-breaking fiasco would be the last time I'd ever suit up for a professional football game again. One percent chance or not, Levette and I both knew that it was time to discover what God had next for me. What would that be? Who knew? Her guess was as good as mine.

Now What?

I was very traumatized by that rib injury, so staying away from football wasn't the hardest thing in the world anymore. That rib breaking still ranks as the number one worst pain I've ever felt in my life. My focus shifted away from playing football and more towards coaching it from time to time at a local high school. But I still needed to choose that major career path that could take care of myself and my family.

I had a sociology degree, I loved working with people, and I loved fitness. So I decided to put all of these aspects together and use my skill sets to start my own personal training business. I started off by going house to house, doing in-person training. I'd take clients to parks, schools, or any facility that would legally allow me to train my growing clientele. My goal was to get my own facility. But facility or not, Triumph Fitness Personal Training in Louisville, Kentucky, was born. This marked another milestone for me, as I'd officially became a small business owner. I was really proud of myself, and my wife was extremely proud of me too.

I always loved seeing her look at me with that proud smile, that look of support and encouragement. Finally, it was much easier for her to look at me this way. I was taking care of her in the way that she deserved to be cared for, the way her mom and dad would have approved of, and the way God would want me to. She championed most of my goals and was always involved in the planning process. "I love you, and I am so proud of you," she'd regularly say. I knew this was also her way of saying that she felt secure and that she trusted me as a praying man of God who would never lead her astray. She watched me make wise investments, decisions, and improvements to our life. She saw that I finally learned how to be willing to roll up my sleeves and work hard even if the task wasn't my favorite. This was so important because for a while, she didn't think that I would know what to do with myself apart from football. She would tell you today that her greatest fear back in the day was that I would never be able to move forward if I didn't get to the NFL at some point.

That was the old me, though. The new me saw things completely differently. Yes, admittedly, a small piece of me still wanted to play, but I wanted us to be stable and secure first and foremost. My mind was on more important things, such as taking care of my family and my personal training business. I began networking, trying to grow the Triumph Fitness brand as best I could. I continued to be active in FCA, coaching, teaching at church, and raising my children. I was handling my business pretty well. I was not yet satisfied, but I was well on my way.

Now you're not going to believe this (or maybe you will), but remember that little 1 percent? Well, when you are healed, you think slightly different than when you are writhing in pain or rehabbing. My agent asked me if I was done with football, and I told him yes. *But*—if someone ever called with an offer, I'd definitely "at least listen." And honestly, part of me started to hope again. I, for sure, would not have minded at all if my phone would've suddenly rung and the NFL or CFL were on the other end. C'mon. I'm human. (You're probably thinking, *No, you're just hard-headed.* At the time, my wife might've agreed with you!) A really, really, really microscopic smidgen of hope sat in my heart. Not enough to pursue football but enough to at least take a call. A mustard seed of hope. But we all know what can happen to mustard seeds. I think this is where God was like, *Okay. T.C. is just innocently crazy. Let me gracefully reroute him before he gets on another football field and I have to pull his body apart.*

A CHANGE OF PASSION

Of course, I don't think God actually felt like that. But I do feel like he knew that I was ripe for a revealing of his next set of plans for my life. I was ready to have a seed planted in me that would burst and help me change my passions completely to something else. Whatever God felt, I don't think what happened next was a coincidence at all. And I know for sure the next set of events was directly from God. Divine intervention and inspiration at its best. I may have been stubborn, ambitious, and a risk-taker at times. But I never stopped praying. And that always kept me in a position to keep God in the lead, out front, where he belonged. Now when he wants my attention, it's a lot easier for me to recognize the prompting—and give it to him.

Validating My Calling

A few months later while I was driving, I heard an advertisement on a Christian radio station about an acting competition called the AMTC (Actors, Models, and Talent for Christ). I had never heard of a faith-based talent competition quite like this. Actors from all over the country would get a chance to perform in front of legit Hollywood movie companies. There would also be agents in the audience judging the competition. Many performers currently in Hollywood got their start at the AMTC. If this was not enough, I heard that the Kendrick Brothers and Sherwood Pictures would be casting for their next feature film (*Courageous*) at this competition! In my opinion at that time, there could not have been a clearer sign from the Lord than all of this.

When I got home that evening, I shared this information with Levette. We went online and discovered all the information needed to audition. AMTC auditions were being held in various locations around the country, and the competition itself would be held several months later in Orlando, Florida. We quickly began to look for the nearest audition in our region. And we found one right there in Louisville. A few weeks later I went to the audition and was selected as a competitor. Contestants were responsible for their own transportation, hotel, and food. So this would be a costly investment. I raised the money necessary to fund my seven-day stay in Orlando, and I was officially on my way to the AMTC and hopefully on a collision course with the Kendrick Brothers and Sherwood Pictures.

So Close That I Could Touch It

When I got to the AMTC, it was everything that I hoped it would be. I was surprised at how many actors and other performers were there—almost one thousand. I was contestant number 561. A few hundred male actors were in my category. After the seven days were up and all the dust settled, I had won runner-up for the title of best overall male actor. This was an incredible feat for me, and much more than I had expected to happen. I had no formal training, no acting classes, and was dependent only on the AMTC affiliated agency that helped prepare competitors for the showcase. At the end of the competition, competitors would get an envelope with a list of agents and managers that had requested a meeting (this is referred to as a "callback"). These were all of the agents, managers, directors, producers, and major entertainment entities that were watching and judging the talent.

I would have been happy with just one meeting. One callback. And I hoped it would be the Kendrick Brothers. I did get a callback; in fact, I ended up with eleven! But none of them was the one that I wanted. Day seven of the AMTC was all about networking with your callbacks. I went to all eleven meetings and tried to be excited as I could, but my heart was not in it. It's amazing how all of the success from my time in Orlando was starting to feel less fulfilling. I was grateful that I nearly won the whole thing, and I was grateful for the eleven callbacks (some people did not get any). But there was just something very deflating about not getting the attention of Sherwood Pictures and having the opportunity to audition for their upcoming film *Courageous*.

But later, I found out that the casting representatives for the film would not have called me for a meeting anyway because they were casting for teenage roles—not adults. That was bittersweet news. At least I could take comfort in knowing it wasn't my performance that didn't get me a Sherwood Pictures callback with the Kendricks. They weren't looking for my type. But that also meant that no adult roles would be cast for their film at the AMTC, so the likelihood of me at least getting to meet them and introduce myself went flying out the window. This was disappointing.

After I finished my eleventh and final callback meeting, I walked out of the conference room, and to my right I saw a very encouraging sight. It was Erin Bethea, the lead actress from *Fireproof*. The thought that immediately popped into my head was that I had to talk to her. There was no way that she wouldn't know how to get me in contact with the Kendricks. She was surrounded by media, so I had to wait patiently. Meanwhile as the runner-up for best overall male actor, I had apparently gained a few new fans because people started to come up to me for autographs. Humbled, I gladly took the moment and signed as many as I could. Once I got finished and looked up—Erin was gone! You had to be kidding me. I was so close to Erin that I could practically reach out and touch her, and I just let her slip away. I continued to look for Erin and had no luck. I could not believe I had just let that happen.

When I returned to Louisville, I decided to try one more thing. Since Erin was at least in attendance and everyone in the building comes to the awards ceremony, I was certain that she may have seen how well I did. I thought maybe she would remember contestant number 561—the guy who nearly won the whole thing. I scoured the internet to try and find her email, and I did.

I proceeded to write an email to Erin that was so long even I would have skipped it if I were her. I poured out my heart and told her how much I loved *Fireproof*, mainly for the impact that it had on other people. Throughout this long email, I let her know that my desire was to become a professional actor who could bring glory to God within the entertainment industry. I told her that I thought my only opportunity to do this would be with the Kendricks because no one else I knew was making movies with a God-first mentality the way they were. There was nothing that I wanted more than to be a part of this kind of ministry that had the potential to change the lives of millions of people around the world.

I finally wrapped everything up by reminding her of my number—contestant 561—and I hoped that she remembered me. When I sent this email, I didn't know if she'd ever get it. If she did get it, I didn't think she'd ever read it. But both happened. She got it and read it—each and every word! Erin told me that she had gotten emails like mine all the time, but there was something different about the one I sent. She said that for whatever reason, mine just jumped out. She read everything that I had to say and felt the heart behind it. She forwarded my information and email over to her father and mother—who just so happened to be the executive producer and casting director for Sherwood Pictures—Pastor Michael Catt and his wife, Terri Catt. So after a few discussions amongst themselves and eventually the Kendrick brothers, the decision was made to reach out to me for an audition.

I will never forget where I was or what I was doing when Terri Catt called me from Albany, Georgia. I was driving home from a personal training session when my cellphone screen displayed an area code that I was unfamiliar with. When I answered the phone and Terri introduced herself, I got extremely excited. She told me that she had read my email and that there could be a role for me. She said that she was going to be sending me a few lines from the new movie *Courageous* and asked if I could put something on tape as soon as possible. I immediately went home and downloaded the lines. I went into my garage to set up my scene. The character was a very dangerous and mean gang leader by the name of "T.J.," and in this scene, he was threatening everyone in his car. The scene ends with T.J. pulling out a shotgun and nearly shooting a cop in the chest.

I pulled together a few chairs to create my car. I did not have a gun or anything that resembled a gun, so I used a small black baseball bat as my shotgun. Then I told Levette to press record on my camera and gave the best performance that I felt that I could do.

The Callback I *Really* Wanted

A few days later, Terri called again. I had her number saved, so when I saw the name, my heart leaped with excitement. I'm not sure why because she could have been calling to say that she didn't like it. But when I answered the phone, I discovered that everyone loved my initial audition. The next step was to do an in-person audition, but there was not enough time for me to figure out a way to get to Albany, Georgia, with such short notice.

Terri suggested that I do an audition via Skype. I honestly had never heard of Skype at the time, but I found out how to use it really quickly. I went home and immediately set up my Skype account, and in the coming days I did something that I had never done before in my life: audition for my first major film role while sitting on my living room couch.

When the audition day arrived, I was very nervous. I was sitting there on the couch with everything setup. My Skype account was open, and the webcam was pointed right at me. I've got a bottled water sitting on the floor nearby, and I'm just trying to stay calm. Levette made sure that I was all alone and everything was quiet. Relaxing was tough, and my heart was beating up into my ears. As I was checking my Skype to make sure I was online, the Skype call from Sherwood Pictures came in suddenly—and scared me like crazy. I composed myself as quickly as I possibly could. This was it. I answered the call, and Terri Catt appeared on the screen. Seeing her warm smile and kind eyes made my anxiety come down quite a bit. She then panned the camera back to a wider view, revealing everyone else in the room: Alex Kendrick, Stephen Kendrick, and a bunch of others staring right at me. My anxiety went right back up!

Alex and Stephen began to tell me how the audition was going to go. They asked me if I was ready, and I said yes while attempting to readjust my camera. I'm not sure what happened, but suddenly my screen went black (as if my computer had gone to sleep). I kept quiet, but I immediately panicked! I thought I had lost them, but then I could still hear their voices. I was trying to figure out how to get things back on so I could see them, and I kept running my mouse across the mouse pad to try to wake up my laptop.

"Can you see me okay?" I asked, trying to keep the panic out of my voice. They told me that they could see me just fine, so I started to relax. This was good.

Finally, my computer woke up, and Alex started the scene. Rather than look at the computer screen and the people in the room, I just stared at the webcam, not even seeing any of them at all, which calmed me down greatly. I tried to give the most convincing performance I possibly could and bring the T.J. character to life. When the audition was done, they thanked me for taking the time to audition and told me that they would be making their decisions according to how God leads. And that was it. All I could do now was wait.

Receiving a Different Kind of Call

Weeks had gone by, and I still had not heard anything from Sherwood Pictures or the Kendricks. I was happy that I still had quite a bit to keep me busy. But no matter what I was doing, I kept waiting for the phone to ring, hoping it would be some great news about the role of T.J. I realized that I wasn't even looking for a call from my football agent anymore. One percent of hope was basically the equivalent of an NFL dream that was on life support, barely hanging on. Forget football right now—I really wanted to be in this movie!

Meanwhile my personal training business was doing well. My days of running house to house were about to end. With enough money saved (combined with a small loan), I was able to begin renting a large warehouse space. Triumph Fitness Personal Training was now a two thousand square foot facility. I will never forget the day we received our keys. The place was dusty, dirty, and needed a ton of work. But Levette and I were up for the challenge. We scrubbed every foot of that building. We painted the walls and the floors. We painted some of our favorite Scripture verses along the walls.

Levette put her engineering and artistic abilities to fantastic use by bringing to life my mental design for the company logo. Together we painted black letters "T" and "F" twenty feet high on an already freshly painted white wall. Four feet from the floor, we added a sporty red stripe along the wall, running it throughout the entire facility. We put polyurethane on a freshly painted, all-black floor. The shine from the lights above was awesome. We installed a few AC units, lit some candles, decorated the foyer and seating area, and then we decorated the main office. A few days later, all of the fitness equipment was delivered. It was beautiful. Everything was beautiful. Best of all was how Levette and I did it together. We made a great team. We still do.

Man, I was so proud.

I continued to perform with KidWay, volunteer as a Sunday school teacher, and coach high school football. But again, it didn't matter what I was doing because my mind was wondering if or when the phone would ring. The teeter-totter nature of an athlete is fascinating. We flip-flop so much! I just decided to look at it this way: playing football would always be something that would flash in my head, most likely until the day came when it would be physically impossible for me to play. And even that would be subjective. Case in point, even though I knew chances might be slim that I would ever play for the NFL, it was hard to *not* think about getting *that call.*

I Got A Call

Finally, one day, the phone did ring. But it had nothing to do with football. I was still in the process of packing and moving to the new fitness facility. I answered the phone, and it was Alex Kendrick. Of course, I was extremely excited and assumed that I had gotten the role of T.J. But that wasn't why he called. Instead, this was a spirituality check. Alex was calling me to ask me about my walk with Jesus. I loved this about him. Alex and Stephen cared about my relationship with Jesus above everything else. Yes, they wanted to get an actor, but they wanted that actor to be right with God. I truly respected that. He did not mention whether I had been chosen for the role of T.J. or not because this call was more about who I was as a man.

So when the call was over, the wait resumed. I wasn't offered the role just yet, but I wasn't rejected either. I was still in the running. As the weeks went on, I would receive a couple more calls letting me know that I was still being considered. Continuing my normal routine helped waiting get easier and easier.

Never Saw It Coming

Part of my normal routine included playing basketball every Wednesday morning at 6:00. Several of us would meet at the church gym and run full court games for about two hours. One Wednesday morning, I got up like I always did at 5:00 a.m. and grabbed my gym bag. I stopped at the same gas station to get the same energy drink that I would always get. This gas station was directly across the street from the church parking lot. I would always buy two energy drinks, drink one full one before we started playing, and then drink the other one a bit later. We athletes are big about sticking to our routines.

But as I pulled out of the gas station on my way to the church across the street, a van going at highway speed crashed into the SUV that I was driving. I never saw it coming. The van smacked into the right front end of my vehicle and sent it spinning in place. I was knocked out of my seat and into the passenger seat. This accident didn't seem real, and for a moment, I thought that I was dreaming. When everything stopped spinning, I accepted the reality of the moment, composed myself, and then exited my mangled SUV. A short time later, the police, fire department, and ambulance all arrived. Thankfully, no one sustained any life-threatening injuries.

Shock is probably the best word to describe my state of mind as I stood at the crash site. Moments later my wife and children arrived on the scene. They saw the wreckage and obviously were grateful that I was alive. After talking with the police, the other driver, and other bystanders who wanted to make sure that I was okay, I began to have my own interesting thought. I imagined what would have happened had I died. I asked myself if I was ready to meet Jesus, if this was it.

I became very uncomfortable with myself because the answer seemed to be *no.* I didn't think I was ready. And this wasn't the "not wanting to die" kind of ready. Most people are understandably *not* ready for that. I'm talking about the kind of ready that Jesus says we need to be. Was I living my life the way he wanted me to? I had read in Scripture where Jesus says in Matthew 7:21 (NLT) that "Not everyone who calls out to me, 'Lord! Lord!' will enter the Kingdom of Heaven. Only those who actually do the will of my Father in heaven will enter."

Right there, standing at that wreckage, I imagined having been killed in the crash—and then standing face-to-face with Jesus Christ. I imagined Jesus asking me if I had been living life according to my will or God's will. I wanted my answer to be a definite, "Yes—it has been God's will." But for whatever reason, as spiritually mature as I had become, I did not believe that "God's will" would have been my answer. I honestly felt like I had an off-and-on relationship with God's will. I didn't like the possibility that I was only interested in what God wanted whenever I got confused about *what I wanted*. Because I knew that when whatever I wanted to do with my life was working, and it wasn't hurting anybody, and it was positive, I was okay to do it. But what if that was not what God wanted me to do? What if I was only following my will, not his?

I realized that having my plans work or be successful could not be the criteria for determining if I was doing God's will. And doing something positive may not seem like something that would be displeasing to God, but I learned from Scripture not to think with human logic. There are a lot of people who do that and who will one day hear Jesus say, "I never knew you. Away from me" (v. 23 NIV). And I assure you that they logically were expecting to hear something else. I did not want this to be me.

So that same day, I made a promise to myself and my family that I would never put anything above pursuing God's will for my life. I told them that I was always going to hold them accountable for doing the same thing. I asked everyone to commit to never wasting a day because we never know when we might be breathing our last breath. I told them that I never wanted them to forget this fact: either by death or by Christ's return, we all have a guaranteed meeting with Jesus someday—and we never know when that day will be. I refused to lead myself or anybody in my family away from their God-given purpose in life. I truly believed that this was what God wanted me to take away from this moment. Of all the calls that I had been hoping to get, this was the one that I actually needed: *a wakeup call*. I had been telling myself to study more, pray more, and prioritize making disciples. But I would always procrastinate, banking on getting started another day. Now I realized that we never know if tomorrow is a day that we will ever see, making it unwise to put off anything that God has purposed me (or you) to do.

To make sure that I'd never forget the lesson learned from this near-death experience, I kept my totaled SUV's keyless entry remote from the crash and made it into a necklace. I've been wearing that remote around my neck ever since.

One week after the accident, I received yet another phone call from Alex Kendrick. And finally, after weeks of waiting, I was officially offered the role of T.J. in the fourth Kendrick Brother's film, *Courageous*! The timing could not have been better. It seemed as though everything that I had gone through and learned was positioning and preparing me for this very moment. I was blown away. I called Levette and broke the news. She screamed with excitement, and we both praised God together.

Courageous

Once it had finally dawned on me that I was *really* about to take on a major movie role, it was time to start learning my lines and packing my bags for Albany, Georgia. It was truly a surreal feeling to know that I was headed to work with Sherwood Pictures when less than two years prior, I had been moved to tears by *Fireproof*. With *Fireproof*, I was particularly affected by Ken Bevel's role. Oddly enough, when I finally arrived in Albany and was immediately driven to the set to meet the

Sherwood Pictures team, the first actor I met was Ken Bevel. Ken was shooting the gun range scene from *Courageous*. As I watched, everything became even more of a reality for me. *I'm about to be in a movie!*

When I went back to my hotel that night, there were so many thoughts running through my mind. To my surprise, I started to feel a crazy amount of pressure. I started to remind myself that I had never done this before. I had no training, no acting coaches, no references. Yet somehow, I was just going to head up to the set on day one and crush it? What would constitute "crushing it" anyway? This wasn't a reality TV show. This was the real deal. This wasn't a stage show at church. This was a theatrical movie that the *world* would see.

For sure, I started to have a few doubts. I didn't want to fail. While at the set earlier that day, I had met Ken Bevel, Alex Kendrick, Stephen Kendrick, Pastor Michael Catt and his wife Terri, and Erin Bethea. Collectively, these were all the people responsible for my casting. They told me how difficult it had been to cast my character—a cruel and dangerous thug—and the actor who played him needed to convince the audience that he was completely immoral. The audience needed to fear and hate this character at the same time. They needed to believe that I was "T.J."—a ruthless, heartless gangbanger. If the audience could be convinced of all of this, it would play a huge role in the film's overall success.

While the role of T.J. was small, it was also a key part of the film's message. Other than sin itself, T.J. was the main antagonist. Alex and Stephen expressed great confidence in me that I could pull off what was necessary to bring the character to life despite having never seen me act other than my audition tape. I felt extremely encouraged by the faith that they had in me. In their own words, they let me know that I was an answered prayer concerning the role. Honestly, that made me nervous. Not so much the answered prayer part, because I believed that too. It was the high hopes and high expectations that began to weigh on me. My audition tape was strong, so everyone was expecting me to live up to it and even take it to another level. With such a polarizing character, a lackluster or underwhelming delivery was easily possible. I certainly did not want anyone to regret casting me. In my mind, I thought about how bad it would be for critics to review *Courageous* and love the film but hate me. I imagined them saying something like, "*Courageous* was one of the Kendricks' best films yet. Great acting all around, *except for the gang leader portrayal.* Stallings was not very believable at all. His rawness was evident. I wasn't convinced."

I couldn't help myself. I was literally imagining my own negative reviews and write-ups of my performance. I can't overstate the fact that I had *no* formal actor training. No classes. No coaching. No experience, and no previous methods to lean on. No relaxation techniques or anything. Because that fact makes the rest of the story beautiful. I didn't need it. Those things would come into play much later in my career, but on this day, for this role, I didn't need anything but Jesus. God would get all the glory. Not me, not training or techniques. God was all I had. God and the gifts that he had given me.

Quiet on the Set!

Sleep the night before my first day on set was hard to come by. Morning came quickly, and the next thing I knew, I was in hair and makeup. They began to transform me into the T.J. character by darkening my overall complexion and adding gang tattoos. I began to do several push-ups to get the blood flowing. T.J. was an evil dude. I needed to get myself into that mindset. At least I knew to do that much. I couldn't be a menacing gang leader with a big T.C. Stallings smile on my face.

My personality was completely different from my character's demeanor. I knew that if I were able to pull this off, it could really send a strong message to the world about my skills. The opposite was also true. It might be the last role I ever got if I bombed. Positive and negative thoughts continued to compete in my head. Once the makeup session ended, I took a look in the mirror. I definitely looked the part, with tattoos on my neck and my arms and chest still pumping from the push-ups. I looked convincing. But could I *be* convincing? We would soon find out. But first, it was time to go back to the wardrobe area and get dressed.

After putting on the denim jeans and some big black boots, I tied a black bandana to my left bicep. I placed a large diamond studded chain around my neck, along with diamond earrings, and a huge silver wristwatch. I slipped into a tight, black muscle shirt and tucked it into my jeans, which were held together by a thick black belt with a large silver buckle. Finally, I tied on the black durag to complete the look. I dropped my eyebrows low, putting on an intimidating scowl.

Keeping it on my face, I walked over to the mirror. Pretty much scared myself. I wasn't T.C. anymore. I was definitely "T.J. the gang leader" now.

And...I was still *crazy nervous.*

Another Milestone

When I arrived on set for my first official scene, I felt so blessed. I was officially a professional actor about to make history in my family as soon as someone called *"Action!"* Growing up, so many people dream about moments like this, and now—for me—it was a reality. I was so nervous though. But it was time to put up or shut up.

I've kept saying how I had not one ounce of actor training, but I mean it when I tell people that I believe God was coaching me. I did some very effective things instinctively that helped me prepare to be T.J. After all the handshaking and compliments on how "real and believable I looked," I went off and sat alone in the corner of a nearby room. Alone. I closed my eyes and dropped my head, going into deep thought and prayer. After asking God to be with me as I attempted to do my best, I went into a long period of reflection.

I needed to get angry, and fast. So I began to think about things that made me as upset as I could tolerate. I thought about my childhood and all the times I felt hurt. I blocked out anything good, making room only for anything that disappointed me. I recalled any family drama, all the gang violence, the drive-by shootings, the hood fights, the drug dealers— all of it. Any failures, disappointments, any individuals that had ever wronged me—I remembered them at this moment.

I dwelled on all of this negativity for so long that by the time they brought me back to set and called "action," I was *more* than ready.

When we wrapped for the day, I was showered with compliments. It was clear to me that I had gotten off to a great start, and I knew who T.J. was. That scene set the stage for the rest of my performance. When it was all said and done, I had accomplished much more than simply *looking* the part. According to everyone in the cast and crew, I had embraced the role of T.J.—and given *Courageous* the villain it needed (and what the Kendricks had hoped for). I was extremely humbled by the entire experience.

Still, none of it felt real until the day *Courageous* hit theaters in the fall of 2011. The film opened at number four in the nation, and my acting career had officially begun. The only thing left for me to do was read the reviews and see if the world felt as good about my performance as the cast and crew did. To my relief, I never saw the nightmare write-up that I imagined I'd see. Nobody accused me of being "not believable." In fact, it was quite the opposite. Those who didn't know me swore that I was a reformed gang member. If that wasn't enough, a few days later, I was crossing paths with a lady and her young daughter. Apparently, they recognized me from the film, and the daughter hid behind her mother as they passed by! The mom even went as far as to put some distance between themselves and me. True story. And of course, I took that as a compliment. The actor in me now began to get hungry in much the same way that the athlete used to be. *Courageous* was a fantastic experience. But now, I wanted more.

Aside from my newfound acting confidence and a new relationship with Sherwood Pictures, there was another very cool residual effect from doing *Courageous*. I found some healing. It came in the form of conviction, and this conviction led to action. With *Courageous* being about fatherhood and forgiveness, I found it hypocritical that I had never made an attempt to reconnect with my own father and practice what the filmed preached. So after filming, I did just that. We connected for a face-to-face meeting, and I buried any resentment right then and there. I truly forgave him, and I hope he forgave himself. Only he truly knows that.

Chapter 11

IS THIS A JOKE?

After *Courageous* opened in theaters, life changed a little—but not that much. It was crazy to see myself on the big screen, and part of me was thinking that now, suddenly I was going to be bombarded by paparazzi or crazy screaming fans. But that didn't happen. There may have been a fan or two every now and again, and of course everyone who knew me personally had something to say. But this wasn't Hollywood. I was still living in Louisville, Kentucky. Once that reality set in, it became easier to handle the fact that I was truly an actor. My head didn't get too big. I went back to work at my personal training studio. I kept coaching, kept teaching and acting at church, and just kept being me. There was no need to think much more of my newfound career. It's not like Hollywood was going to come calling.

Hollywood Comes Calling

I absolutely 100 percent thought it was a joke, but the area code was definitely a Southern California number. When the caller told me her name and the agency that she was with,

Levette and I immediately looked it up while we were talking to her. Sure enough, there she was. Kim Dorr of Defining Artists Agency. This was really happening. I was talking to a Hollywood agent just weeks after Courageous was released. I had to calm myself down so that I could stop thinking it was a joke and really listen to what she had to say.

It turned out that Kim was actually in church ministry as well as entertainment. She also ran an acting ministry at her church in which she would mentor actors in Hollywood. Now if I was going to have an agent, it definitely needed to be someone like Kim. I in no way saw her reaching out to me as an accident. This was who God wanted me to connect with. The only problem was—I didn't believe that right away.

Kim made every effort to let me know that her agency respected the type of person that I was, the type of standards that I had, and that they would do their very best to find me the kind of roles I wanted. She also told me that the only way this would work was if I lived in LA. Now things just got real. I couldn't even wrap my mind around something like this. Move to Los Angeles? Honestly, once Kim said that I would have to move to California, my excitement about the whole call went completely down the tubes. I didn't know the first thing about pulling off such a relocation. Instantly the whole idea just became stupid. I was flattered but refused to give it any more thought.

Although God had truly matured me as a Christian, we all still have our flaws with which we must work on correcting daily. I mentioned that one of my biggest problems was pro-crastination, but the only thing worse than procrastination is not knowing that you're procrastinating in the first place. The proper thing to do with this whole Hollywood thing was put it into prayer and let God sort it out. Kim had given me until the end of the year to make a decision—roughly ninety days away. She did not say that I needed to be fully relocated by then, but she at least wanted to know whether or not relocation was a possibility for me.

I looked at three months as plenty of time to think this over. So I didn't even address it in my prayers right away. Success in other areas of my life also enabled me to procrastinate. My personal training business was going well. My marriage was great. My kids were healthy. I loved teaching at the church. I was in no hurry to rack my brain over trying to figure out how to move to Hollywood. God probably knew that I would never get around to talking to him about this. Part of me believes that he began to do specific things to get my attention so that I *would* pray about the relocation. Whether he did that or not, that's exactly what ended up happening anyway. Circumstances out of my control began to bring me to my knees.

As a new business owner, I was still learning lessons by trial and error. A lesson that I was beginning to learn very quickly was that it was much too hard to handle the cost of maintaining two rental properties. Between our home and our personal training studio, the rents alone were costing me thousands per month. My clientele at the studio were great, and I was making good money, but with the cost to run everything, we were barely breaking even. I was basically paying to be in business.

As with any business, there would be slow periods. For me, it usually was the summer because not very many people were signing up for memberships or training due to vacations. The other slow time would be late fall to early winter. This is the time where all of the "eating holidays" fall (Thanksgiving and Christmas dinners and New Year's Eve pre-resolution feast fests), so usually, no one was thinking about personal training or wanting to hear about healthy choices (even I didn't want to hear it!).

But our bills did not care about a slow season—they just wanted to be paid. And for the first time since opening the studio, I began to seriously struggle. This was tough because we had a lot of regular clients, and the gym was always bustling. It looked much more successful than what it really was. Eventually, we had a decision to make. We could no longer afford both rental properties. Either the home or the business had to go. After talking things through with Levette and praying for wisdom, the most sensible thing to do was to give up the home. At least with the business, we had a way to make money. So the fairly large office at my personal training studio became the new address for the Stallings family home. Technically, we were homeless.

Fear

There was one client that I would train at 5:00 a.m. Normally this would not be an issue, but now my whole family was asleep in my office. We hadn't told anyone that we were living at the studio. Part of the reason we kept it a secret was embarrassment, but most of it was the desire to prevent distractions from the business growing. We knew that by not renewing our home lease, we could begin saving the rent money. The great unknown was whether living in our studio was actually a practical long-term possibility until we saved enough money to do something different. The answer to that question would come rather quickly.

It didn't take but a few days to come the conclusion that our fitness studio was not the answer. At best, it could serve as a temporary bandage to stop the bleeding. Living at the studio was simply much too difficult for several reasons. We were sandwiched between two warehouses, so we could never control the noise around us. We had no kitchen. My office had a mini refrigerator and a microwave, but that was it. Anything that we would eat had to be microwavable and small enough to fit in our little fridge.

And then there was always the fear that someone would notice that our car never left the studio. We slept on inflatable mattresses, so I also worried that someone would see my family sleeping on the floor one day. We always hoped that no one would ever ask us if we slept there because we were not willing to lie. We would definitely tell the truth and then most likely have too many people worried about our financial health instead of coming to train like normal.

It didn't take long before we grew weary of the new lifestyle. Levette and I both knew that it was time to do something different. We knew the feeling of God trying to get our attention. But what did God want us to do? Or rather, what did God want *me* to do? Could it possibly be this acting thing? I didn't know, and the whole Hollywood idea just felt too unreal to consider.

Can't Get It out of My Head

I tried to put the success of *Courageous* and the surprising phone call from Hollywood out of mind. But I couldn't. At least I tried to keep it in the back of my mind so that I could focus on more important things. That didn't work either. I just had so many questions.

I lay awake one night thinking, "What if *this* happens?" and "What if *that* happens?" It was a weird balance of positive and negative thoughts. After some time, I realized that it had gotten extremely late, and I needed to get some sleep. I had a client that would be showing up at 5 a.m. on the dot. I tried to sleep, but I couldn't. Just kept wondering about the call. Determined to rid my mind of this adrenaline rush, I finally was able to force myself to think about other things.

At some point, I finally drifted off to sleep. But I don't think God wanted me to think about other things. Or maybe I had stressed myself out too much. I can't tell you what the reasoning was, but all I know is that my sleep was short lived. I popped up in the middle of the night thinking about the call. Was God behind that call? Was this a sign? I was so frustrated because I just wanted to sleep. The lack of sleep coupled with the confusion about the phone call eventually gave birth to the absolute worst migraine headache I had ever had in my life. I'm not a crier when it comes to pain, yet this thing brought me to tears.

Levette had begun to sense my struggle and got up to check on me. I told her everything, and she had a simple suggestion. Pray, just like I did with everything else. I told her that the whole thing seemed ridiculous, and I felt silly talking to God about it. Our situation (in my mind) didn't seem to be going in a direction that had room to pursue a Hollywood acting career. She said that was even more reason to seriously talked to the Lord about it. She reminded me that God tends to think differently than we do. Bottom line, praying about it would ensure that we had not left any stone unturned, and it could also lead to some relief of the headache.

She was right. We needed to pray. We gave it to the Lord, no matter how stupid I felt about discussing with God the whole idea of relocation to California. But I did experience a better sense of peace that night. And the headache did die down a bit. Then I slept. Not long, but it was enough.

After a long night of struggling with a massive migraine headache, I had a good session with my early client. Once she left, Levette and I grabbed some coffee and talked things over concerning the call from the Hollywood agent. We discussed the main causes of all my apprehensions. What bothered me the most about this whole situation? It became clear that the main culprit was a strong dose of fear. Fear of the unknown. Fear of failure. Fear of making the wrong decision. Fear of going back to the way things were. This was different from taking risks to pursue the NFL. I was in my wheelhouse then, so fear was the last thing on my mind. But now, we were not talking football here. This whole acting thing was relatively new. Doing it professionally was pretty much foreign to me. It was hard to find a basis of comfort to build my confidence on. *Courageous*? It was a fantastic movie, but my role was small. I wasn't even one of the leads. Nothing about my performance (in my opinion at the time) suggested that I had achieved "stardom" as an actor—especially not enough to consider a life-altering relocation to Hollywood.

Now all kinds of questions began to pop back into my head again. How did I know this wasn't the devil simply trying to sway me into something God never intended for me to do? What becomes of my business if this acting dream fails? I began to rationalize as best I could, but even then, fear was motivating the direction my thoughts would take. There were so many unknowns. I knew I was headed down migraine lane once again if I kept this up.

I started unintentionally playing God's part. It's as though I started answering my own prayers to avoid the process of having to patiently trust God. I convinced myself that I did not need to go to Hollywood to succeed as an actor. I had already made my theatrical debut in a film that went to number four across the country, and I did that from Louisville, Kentucky—not *Hollywood.* Who's to say I couldn't do it again—from right here where I am?

Levette and I both knew where all this talk was coming from. All this overly cautiousness cloaked in responsible thinking really meant I was just scared because such a big move like this—packed with so much uncertainty—took me out of the control position. I didn't have all the answers to the tests before taking it. I didn't have a cheat sheet. I didn't have a study guide. This was mostly a trust situation. A "trust fall" on a level that I had not experienced before. If I ended up getting a yes from God to move over two thousand miles to California, he'd be pushing me away from everything that I knew. I feared going on this journey. I realized I hadn't wanted to keep on praying about Hollywood because I was afraid that God was going to say yes. It was that simple. Coming to that honest assessment helped me to focus and recalibrate. I knew that God hadn't given me a spirit of fear. I didn't need to fear God's will. My real fear needed to be the possibility of missing out on it.

Eventually, I knew better than to fight with God. I didn't want any more migraine headaches. I didn't need any more signs. I didn't want any more warnings. Although I still did not know if God wanted me to make such a drastic move, I did know that I had to pray about it consistently until I felt his clear decision on the matter.

When I prayed, I asked for forgiveness. I asked the Lord to forgive me for thinking that I knew better. I asked him to forgive me for not trusting him. I admitted to God that I was weak when it came to trusting him when things were out of my control. I told him that I realized that this whole Hollywood thing was way over my head. I had already learned from past experiences that God-sized problems are best handled by God.

The more I humbly admitted that fear was the culprit, the more I realized that the fear was coming from Satan, and I refused to allow it to hold me back a day longer. I decided to stop being a slave to fear. Levette and I knew that it was time to be bold and courageous in our prayers and then to back everything up with faithful action. We said a simple prayer:

Lord, if you want us in Hollywood, open the door. If not, please shut it. And give us the wisdom to truly discern your will. We just want to do the right thing.

Once we made this decision, we began to experience a series of days in which we could clearly hear God speak. Signs began to undeniably point to Hollywood. No, we did not hear God audibly or anything sensational like that. We knew what God wanted by the way he answered our consistent prayers. We understood his plans for us through consistently praying and studying Scripture. He also worked his plans for us through the actions of others. In multiple ways, God was making it clear that nothing could stop us from successfully relocating except our own reluctance to have faith and go.

Situation after situation created obstacles which we had no idea how to overcome and which would possibly prevent us from being able to leave, but God took care of it. Roadblock after roadblock, removed. Did any doubt or fear ever creep back in? Yes, many times. However, courage is not the absence of fear but rather the courageous moves that you make by trusting God regardless of the fear. Over time, for me and my family, fear would lose its grip altogether. A consistent, strong, Holy Spirit-led faith took its place. We did not know how God was going to make Hollywood happen; we just knew that our job was to validate the calling with God. After doing that, we no longer cared where God was taking us, just about the fact that *he* was leading.

So on January 1, 2012, my family and I left behind everything we owned and spent our New Year's Day embarking on a new journey. With nothing but our car, our clothes, important documents, and our pet Labrador retriever, we completed a two-day trip from Louisville, Kentucky, to Southern California. The mission was crystal clear: honor God with every role I take and use every gift within me for the glory and honor of Jesus Christ—while leading and encouraging others to do the same.

Hollywood

I arrived in Hollywood focused, committed, and unashamed of the calling. Those who know of me also know that I have done very well for myself in terms of succeeding as an actor. If you don't know me that well, I'll sum it up for you this way:

I came to Hollywood with a clear intention and plan to honor God with my career. I wanted to make it to the top without forgetting to follow Jesus the entire way. I didn't want to ever compromise my beliefs, ignore Scripture, or use sinful means to gain *any* measure of success. Satan consistently tempted me to abandon the plan, but the grace of God always kept me upright and strong. Then, after three years of trusting in, walking with, and staying behind Jesus, I woke up one day as the lead actor in the *number one* movie in America, *War Room*. It was a movie about prayer. A movie about faith. A movie about courage. A movie about persistence. A movie about *Jesus*. And this all happened in Hollywood—a place where I was almost too afraid to let God take me.

I have been in Southern California now for nine years. Some of my greatest achievements have happened within this time frame. It's no wonder Satan didn't want me to stay the course. By pursuing the plans that God had for me and trusting the process, I ended up being cast in over twenty feature films thus far. I did not plan to do any commercials, but God opened that door too. I've done five now, with two of them featured in prominent events (the Olympics and the Superbowl in 2016).

Freeing myself to follow the plans God had for me, I emptied my work plate, and God filled it up with exciting new things. I became a public speaker and traveled all over the country telling people about Jesus. While I was living in Louisville, I enjoyed teaching around the city and sharing my testimony, but my life was much too busy to even think about leaving the state every week to do the same. With God's new calling on my life, that's exactly what I've been able to do. Almost every week, if I were not auditioning or on a film set, I was in another state sharing Christ.

Speaking of auditions—God was using me in an amazing way when it came to those too.

Auditioning in Hollywood is an interesting process. My fellow actors will know what I am getting at. It has two sides to it. On one hand, it's exciting and fun. Auditions are always an opportunity to learn, to meet new people, and to network. (Sidenote—I was able to meet so many of the actors that I had grown up watching! This was always a welcome part of the experience. It helped remind me that I belonged. I would see a collection of so many great actors and actresses, and then I was invited to the same auditions alongside them. That meant that somebody thought I was good enough to be in the room with elite-level performers. That will certainly put some wind beneath anyone's wings).

Then there is the other side of the audition process. The competitive side. Auditions involve people sizing you up. The tension in the room can be so weird at times. It's pin-drop quiet in some cases, and at other times, the hundreds of people in the room are so noisy that it sounds like a high school cafeteria. I would always see people from all walks of life, all kinds of faiths and beliefs, and each one on some sort of journey. Everyone has a story. If you listened close enough to the conversations around you at a Hollywood audition, that's what you will hear most of the time—somebody talking about their life, about where they were, where they are thinking about going, and the road that brought them to Hollywood. This got me to thinking. I need to jump in on this. I, *for sure,* had a story.

Normally I would never talk to anyone at my auditions. I liked to focus and drown out anything around me. But it never failed that someone would sit next to me and start a conversation. Funny thing is, I had developed a technique to politely avoid this. I'd make myself look as uninteresting a person as possible. The brim of my hat was always pulled low in the front. If I had no hat, then I'd use the hood of my jacket. To add to this and make it more difficult for someone to talk to me, I would wear a pair of headphones. I wouldn't be listening to any music because I would run the risk of not hearing my name called for my turn to audition. But people always assumed that I was listening to music, so why bother me? It was the perfect way to focus without having to come across as a jerk by saying, "I can't talk right now—I'm studying my lines." Yes, I knew it was the truth and that it shouldn't have offended anyone in this situation, but it always sounds mean to people no matter how you say it.

At one audition in particular, my cover up/headphones method did not work. Someone actually recognized me from

War Room. He tapped me on the arm and checked to see if I was the person that he thought I was. I nodded. So as not to be rude, I pulled off my hood, took off my sunglasses and my headphones, and we began to have a conversation. This turned out to be a very interesting conversation, one that would impact the way I treated the audition room from that day on.

Before I get into the conversation we had, let me give you a bit of context and backstory about the weeks and months leading up to the audition. My representation and I would have long talks about the types of auditions that I would be willing to take. Often I would get requests to audition for projects that had too much profanity in the script. For most of the early part of my time in Hollywood, I wouldn't even give these auditions the time of day. But my manager at the time was adamant that I needed to at least show up to the auditions for the sake of networking. I understood that, but there was still the issue of having to audition for a role when I got there. No way I was going to go cussing up a storm for the sake of networking. My manager told me to consider changing some of the words. Change them into something that I could do. As long as I kept the integrity of the script, nobody would care. As he put it, the bottom line was that nobody knew who I was in Hollywood. I could not afford to keep passing on auditions because even if I didn't get picked for a role, at least the casting directors would get to know me. I wouldn't be a fit for their gritty R-rated flick, but maybe I'd be perfect for something else. It made sense.

The next time an audition came my way containing profanity, I agreed to take it on. I printed out the script and proceeded to swap out dirty words for cleaner things that I could say. This proved to be harder than it sounds. Keeping the script's integrity was just as important as keeping mine in this situation. It defeats the purpose if what I say sounds like a completely different scene. Not to mention, "Shut the dang-on door" didn't quite come off as strong as the original. Needless to say, this took some serious work. But after hours and hours of revising it, I had achieved a clean way to be gritty. It still told the story, and I was pretty sure that what I said—while not exactly what was in the script—was more than close enough. It was respectful enough to the script that the writer would not feel offended. But most importantly to me, I eliminated the chance of disrespecting God.

Now let's fast-forward back to the audition. I was sitting there with this revamped script, trying to become as comfortable and as confident as possible with it. That's when the guy tapped me on the shoulder, recognizing me from *War Room*. Off came my hat, glasses, and headphones so that we could talk. The usual small talk that happens at auditions started. We talked about how we individually ended up in Hollywood. We talk about how things had been going in our careers so far. But then, he asked a question: "So, bro—you're the *War Room* guy, right? What are you doing at an audition for something like this? You really about to go in there and say all that?"

When he asked this question, being that he was auditioning for the same character that I was, he assumed that he and I had the same script in hand. I said to him, "No, I'm not going to say that," pointing to his script. "I'm going to say *this*." I handed him my script, which clearly showed the crossed-out profanities replaced with my own choice of words. He was shocked. He asked me why I felt the need to change the words. He wondered why it meant so much to me to avoid profanity and other forms of dirty talk. I told him to think about the question he asked me a few moments ago. "Was I the *War Room* guy?" I asked him how he would have felt about me had he heard me cussing up a storm in my audition. He saw where I was going with it right away. We ended up talking for quite some time. We were both far down the audition list, which allotted plenty of time to chat. I think all of it was by God's design.

It had begun to get close to my time to go in and audition. By this point, he and I had discussed so many things, one of which was my testimony. Many of the things that you have read in my story so far, this guy was able to hear as well. As a fellow actor, he was mostly impressed by the way I committed my career to Jesus. Finally, my name was called. I walked in the audition room and confidently delivered my lines. I was pleased with it. Those present seemed to be fairly pleased. I connected with the casting director for a brief moment, then I left. My mission was accomplished—in more ways than one. As I was going out, the guy that I'd been talking to was going in. He had heard my audition from the door. He nodded in approval. I nodded back as the door shut behind him.

A few minutes passed after my audition ended, and I was walking through the studio backlots. I was close to approaching the security gate by the exit when I heard my name from behind. It was the guy that I had been talking with. He had finished his audition, and then he ran up to catch me before I left. He then told me that what he saw me do at my audition was inspiring. He said that he had never seen someone do that before. He also said that my story was inspiring, and he was impressed with my journey. The last thing he said was, "Don't stop doing it the way that you do."

I told him how encouraged I was by his words; then we shook hands and went our separate ways.

That day remains a special day that I will never forget. It gave me the blueprint for my future in terms of processing my career opportunities. I realized that not everything about my career would be about *my* gain. For example, I was pretty sure that I was not going to get that role. How did I know? Well, there were twenty other guys in the audition room. If just one of them were equally as talented (or better) and, on top of that, completely willing to deliver the profanity-filled lines, then they would be cast. No doubt about it. Which made it clear to me that maybe God had other plans for me at these types of auditions. Because look at what ended up happening! I was able to tell a fellow actor about why I roll with a Jesus-first mentality when it comes to my career. Who's to say that this wasn't the intent all along? After seeing the impact that my words and actions had on this guy, I was excited about getting the chance to do it all over again at the next audition. The only change I made to the plan was that I needed to be sure to pray before agreeing to any audition. Changing the words wasn't more important than knowing if I should even be there in the first place. Nonetheless, when called to go into a gritty situation, I had a plan that would bring God glory. To this day, this is still the blueprint. When approached about any project or situation, I pray for God to open the door or shut it. If he opens it, I pray for him to make sure I serve my purpose in it—whether that means for me to personally gain something from it or not.

I would be remiss if I didn't share with you the times that the blueprint made life tough. You know Satan is not just going to stand idly by and watch me inspire people in Hollywood for Christ without dropping in some temptation. In my case, it was always the temptation to lower my standards so that I could better my chances in Hollywood. Let's just say I needed to stay in prayer.

Sometimes when an audition for a particular TV role would come in, I'd inquire about the potential salary. To try and make it all work was tempting. But due to the type of person that I would have had to become (just to even make a run at it), I knew that kind of money, life-changing money, would never happen. I'd have to say and do some things that would have been really hard to justify. Many of these roles were too dirty to simply "change a word or two." Nonetheless, it was hard to ignore how much money I could have been making. Combine this potential with my dwindling income, and I had the recipe for a quick, sinful compromise. But after all that God had brought me through, I knew better. There was no chance that I would jeopardize my ability to be an ambassador for Christ. I stayed with the blueprint.

Two pressing issues had begun to arise, both centering around money. First, I wasn't working as much as I wanted to, so money was getting a little tight. Two, there was my manager's income. His money was tight as well. Managers consistently evaluate the talent that they represent. He developed a gripe with me that I completely understood. My standards for the type of projects I took started to cause a cordial rift. Highlighting the fact that he was cordial is important for me to say because my manager was always respectful to me. That is rare in many cases in this business. I liked him a lot and respected the way he presented his issue. The bottom line was finances. We actors bring in money. Agents and managers help produce the opportunities to do that. My manager saw me as a guy that could definitely bring in *much* more money— but it would require dropping my standards significantly.

He wasn't lying. When he showed me the types of roles that I was physically fit for and the types of shows and characters that I could take on, I agreed with his assessments. I knew that I could do those things. But that would kill the mission. The mission was to thrive without settling for those things. However, he stressed that his efforts needed to go more towards those that could help him feed his family. That was *his* mission. He was right. For him, he needed actors that would do just about anything. That wasn't me. To his credit though, he would not cut me from his roster (although I know he wanted to). He even told me how close he came to doing as much. But he said he liked and respected me too much to do that. He was a real, solid guy. And for that reason, I did him a favor and released myself from his roster. He needed to be able to fill that spot with someone that he could use. He knew exactly where I was coming from. The last thing he told me was, "T.C., I respect you. You taught me a lot about having integrity in this business." It meant more to me to hear him say that than anything else he had ever said.

I said that I wasn't going to intentionally teach any lessons in this book, but I do feel the need to say this. God is amazing. There has been nothing that I have enjoyed more than to see him orchestrate his plans in my life. I had my ideas about how this whole Hollywood thing would work out, and most of what I thought would happen makes up only a small part of what actually happened. I just wanted to become successful without leaving true obedience to Jesus out of the picture. God's plan was for me to succeed in films, plus commercials, plus networking, plus speaking, plus writing books, plus coaching other Christian actors, and so much more. God didn't just bring me out to Hollywood to be an actor. He increased my platform and strengthened my ability to have an impact on people—*for him.*

Chapter 12

EYES FIXED

As I sit here writing my story for the world to read (which I have very much enjoyed by the way), I almost have this sense of giddiness going on. It's like a, *I wonder what God has next for my life* type of vibe. I have absolutely no clue. But what I do know is that I feel fully prepared for it. Fully equipped. And this excites me. It amazes me how I can have absolutely *no idea* what is around the corner of my life, yet at the same time, I feel completely prepared for it. The peace that surpasses all understanding that Scripture talks about (Philippians 4:7)—that is the result of faith and trust. Not so much in myself, but in the One who is Lord over me—Jesus. The One who is sovereign over it all—God. And the One who comforts and guides me—the Holy Spirit. Those three are always working together for my good. For *your* good too. What a powerful team to have on our side. And *never* forgetting this is one of the many lessons that my life's journey has taught me.

Another is the lesson of control. The surrendering of control to God was hard. Wanting to always be able to personally dictate the outcome of every situation in my life used to be my biggest problem. You can imagine where that comes from. If you have spent most of your life having everything *out* of your control and always dictated to you, and you hated those outcomes, then at some point you will aim to take back control. Once you get it in control and start succeeding at attaining some of the things you want in life and achieving some of your goals, that control becomes even harder to let go. You tighten the grip around *your* life.

That was me. But I have learned that my life, plans, goals, dreams, desires, pursuits, and the control of it all are best left in the hands of God. Nothing in Scripture tells me that I was meant to have control over my life. Everything in Scripture tells me that I belong to God, that he used Jesus to buy me, and he gifted his Spirit to guide me. I've learned to live a life owned by God. He paid for it. It no longer belongs to me. To take control of it would be stealing. I had already done that once in my life. I'm never doing it again. *Lesson learned.*

In fact, speaking of lessons, I'd like to share with you what my own story has taught me.

Embrace the Loneliness

It took me a while to fully appreciate this lesson from life, but I'm glad I finally have. This one isn't always the easiest to do because who likes to feel left out? Passed up? Looked over? Not many people sign up for that. But Christ followers do. Jesus said in Scripture that, "Foxes have holes, and birds of the air have nests, but the Son of Man has nowhere to lay his head" (Matthew 8:20 ESV). While this was a reference to himself, it was also a warning to those who desire to follow him.

This meant that as followers of Christ today, we are more likely to find ourselves unwelcome than celebrated by the world.

It took me quite a while to understand and accept this, but eventually I did. In fact, I learned to embrace it. Jesus himself embraced it, and the more I read about the how and why behind it, the more I am inspired never to change. Jesus emptied himself out of love for you and me and a strong desire to fulfill God's purpose for his life. And whenever he felt weak, God comforted him. The same holds true for me now, in my own life. I am highly motivated to always embrace the loneliness. And when I say "loneliness," I'm not simply talking about the physical state of being by myself in a room. It's more than that. I'm talking about being by myself when I'm the only one in a group, family, job, relationship, or team who is willing to stand on the principles of Scripture. I'm talking about when I am "not the right fit" for an opportunity that I have been working my whole life to achieve, but because I have that "Jesus" in me, it turns people off.

What do you do? Many people choose to compromise at that point. The check is just too big to ignore. The notoriety is just too great to pass up. The chance to fit in and be celebrated is just too tempting to let pass them by. That kind of thinking *almost* had me too. But I realized that greatest thing that I could do for the love Christ showed me on the cross is to say thank you with my life. He embraced loneliness for me, so I depend on him for the strength to give that love right back. And that commitment has resulted in a consistent feeling of knowing God is proud of me. I place more value on hearing the voice of Christ say, "Well done, good and faithful servant" (Matthew 25:23 ESV) than the voice of my peers saying essentially the same thing.

So I never let Satan make me feel like I am missing out on anything he has to offer as I sit on the outside looking in. If my being unaccepted into any situation is due to having a proper relationship with Jesus, then so be it. I've learned over the years that there is no place I'd rather be than planted firmly within the will of God.

God-ordained Goals

We live in such a "do you" society that makes it hard to trust God with our goal setting, dreams, desires, and pursuits. Social media has given us the ability to look at what someone else is doing, twenty-four hours a day. I used to be naïve about the power of social media until I realized how influential it is. It can cause you to begin setting goals for yourself that you never intended to do. I remember browsing on social media, and I saw video of a guy cutting his own hair. Right away I decided to learn to cut my own hair too. There isn't anything wrong with this, in and of itself. But it did take hours and hours out of my day. Was I going to be a barber one day? A hairstylist? No. Yet I spent the day dealing with my hair for a lot longer than I needed to be. Then I realized that his clippers were much better than mine. Now I wanted new clippers too. You see where this is going.

The point here is that I learned to pray about literally everything. How I spend my time became something that I exclusively wanted the Lord to define. Each and every day. Psalm 139:16 became a Scripture verse that completely changed my life when I read it. When you read it, you will clearly see that before you were born, God already had plans for your life:

> You saw me before I was born.
> Every day of my life
> was recorded in your book.
> Every moment was laid out
> before a single day had passed. (NLT)

I took that personally. His plans were designed with *his* goals for my life in mind. My goals should then consist of these plans. God's plans—not mine. And a beautiful thing happens when you trust this structure. *You succeed.* It's not always pretty or painless. You don't always understand the method behind the madness. You don't always know who the Lord will use to keep you on your path. But what you do know is that a God goal cannot be stopped. This is one of the most encouraging things about my life and story. I hope that this encourages you today.

I live each and every day aiming to ensure that my goals are directly in alignment with God's plans for my life. The way to do this is so simple. In my prayers, I always ask God to guide my day, my mind, my goals, dreams, and desires. My pursuits, planning, and procedures. I beg him to help me make sure that my goals are God-led, God ordained goals. Once I am sure that the path I am on is the one that God has laid out for me, I enthusiastically *run* with it. I may not know how the race will go, but I always know that I will finish it with success. It's a God goal. His plan. Nobody can stop it.

So why would I set goals for myself based on anything else? Satan would love for me to do that. Then he has a chance to put a stop to it. Or worse, he has the chance to help me succeed at pursuing a goal that God never intended for me to put my time, energy, and resources into. Anything to bump me off my God-ordained purpose in life. I'm so glad that I became aware of this. These days, the goal is to always run my plans through God for approval.

Prioritizing Time with God

I have the same routine nearly every single morning of my life. First thing in the morning, I grab coffee and read Scripture for about an hour. I have a prayer board that helps me organize my thoughts. (Yes, I actually do have a "war room" and a prayer strategy.) Time with God is an absolute *must* for me (and for everyone), and I learned throughout these last several years that it's one of the main things Satan tries to rob me of. He will do the same to you, too, if you are aiming to spend a significant amount of time in Scripture and prayer. It's the easiest way to get us focused on the wrong things. The longer I spend time away from God, the less time and opportunity he will have to train me. That's how I look at my time with God, like training sessions. Coaching sessions. As a former professional athlete, this comes so natural to me. I tend to look at God as my coach. I'm the player. The game is life, and Satan is the opponent. I don't want to play the game without my coach consistently giving me the game plan. Uninterrupted time with the Lord is the key to living for him. For me, this is non-negotiable. It's essential, like food and water. I'd even go as far as to say, "like oxygen." I always aim to prioritize time with God this way. Life has taught me that it's a *must* for a Christ follower.

Fear God

"Fear of the Lord is the beginning of wisdom" (Proverbs 9:10 NKJV). And my life has taught me that fearing God is also the way to *stay* wise. Living with a steady, reverent, holy fear of God might be the single most powerful weapon against Satan that I lean on. For me, it's like when I was a child. I feared my mother. Not the way you would fear harm or danger. My mother would never abuse me or anything. But if need be, she would not hesitate to discipline me. So I'm talking about that standard fear that most kids have of getting caught doing the wrong thing. In one way or another, discipline is *not* something most kids want. For me, that spanking or that long, boring punishment created enough of a deterrent from doing wrong. The fear of getting caught, at least in my case, kept me from making the wrong choices most of the time. If fearing a human kept me out of plenty of trouble, how much more effective is the fear of a Holy God? And that is why I love reading Scripture—*the whole Bible*. Old and New Testament. By doing so, I get a full and balanced view of who God is. I see all of his holiness and this creates a level of respect that is a billion times greater than any fear I'd have for a human being.

When I am interviewed, one question that I am asked all the time is, "How do you stay so grounded in your faith?" I answer it the same way all the time. I fear God. It's that sim-ple. "I can't do that because my momma might catch me," is simply replaced by, "I can't do that," or "I have to stop doing this right now because *God* is watching." When you truly place God in any room with you and you constantly remind yourself that he is living inside of you by way of the Holy Spirit, it really does become much harder to sin. This has been the key to spiritual integrity for me.

I'm sharing this with you because it is so important. Satan seems to do his best work when we are isolated. By ourselves. The Bible says that Satan "prowls around like a roaring lion seeking someone to devour" (1 Peter 5:8 NASB). Let's look at that literally. When you watch the lions on the nature channels and they go out for a hunt, they are looking for the prey that is off by itself. And if they can't find one, they come up with a plan to push an animal into isolation. Satan seems to do that too. We isolate ourselves with the ability to pull down the shades, close the doors, delete and clear our search and watch histories, and the like. I've done that before. But what changed everything for me was one day realizing that I hadn't escaped the eyes of God. *He was still there.* All I had done was place myself in a room with just him and me. And now I was going to proceed to commit a sin in front of him? This same holy, powerful God that I read about in the Bible? The One who can speak life into existence or speak life *out* of it just the same? No. Not happening. No temptation is worth it. *I feared God.* Of course, the fact that Christ saved my life should have been the sole motivation for avoiding this temptation. But unfortunately, there are times when his love and grace are ignored or taken for granted, and that's when reminding ourselves that the same God that loves us will also punish us becomes a great deterrent.

The Bible promises that when tempted, I will be given a way out (1 Corinthians 10:13), but I have to *want* to take this way out. And the holy fear of God gives me the desire to want out—to *choose to* allow God to strengthen me and beat the temptation rather than to give in to it. Of course, nobody is perfect. I don't claim to be. But I can tell you that with God's help and a proper fear of who he is, I am more of what God wants me to be rather than what Satan tries to lead me to become. And I aim to stay the course, becoming more and more like Christ each day until I am done here. "Fear of the Lord is the beginning of wisdom."

The Eternal Mindset

I have had a grip on this life lesson for quite some time. It's simply living with a mindset that is motivated by the brevity of life and how at any moment, it could end. Life truly is short. Even if you live to be one hundred, that's short compared to eternity. So we get a few years on earth to prepare for eternity. And we don't even know how many of those years we will get in our lifetime. How, then, should each day be spent, knowing that at any moment we could be face-to-face with God? That's the eternal mindset. Living each day as if it could be your last one and being prepared to meet Jesus no matter the day your earthly life stops (either by death or the return of Christ). James 4:13–17 speaks to this:

> Come now, you who say, "Today or
> tomorrow we will go to such and such a

city, and spend a year there and engage
in business and make a profit." Yet you
do not know what your life will be like
tomorrow. For you are just a vapor
that appears for a little while, and then
vanishes away. Instead, you ought to say,
"If the Lord wills, we will live and also
do this or that." But as it is, you boast in
your arrogance; all such boasting is evil.
So for one who knows the right thing to do
and does not do it, for him it is sin. (NASB)

I have lived my life focused on this mindset for some time now, but just recently, my thoughts on this have been amplified even more. This part of my story will be the most recent event that I have discussed with you so far. It happened back in January of 2020.

I received an email to attend a private movie screening. This is a normal occurrence for me, so no surprise here. But when I read the details of the invite, I was pleasantly surprised. This was an extremely high-level event, exclusive to only seventy-five or so attendees. Many "A-listers" were scheduled to attend. I can humbly say that I was not an A-lister. I was not a Hollywood insider, yet I was invited to attend this very small, intimate movie screening. The movie was *Just Mercy*, featuring a star-studded cast—and all of them were scheduled to attend.

The event was to include a meet and greet, photographs with the cast members, and of course, the pre-screening of the film before it was released to the public. I was extremely flattered to receive an invite, as I could only imagine how many others probably wanted a seat at this screening. And after seeing the name of one of the sponsors, I was almost certain the event was coveted (especially for Los Angeles Lakers fans). That sponsor was Kobe Bryant. Now, I am not a Lakers fan. But I have always been a fan of greatness, no matter my personal attachment. Kobe Bryant was beyond great. As an athlete myself, it was an added bonus to have the opportunity to meet such an iconic player. This had the makings of quite the night.

When my wife and I first arrived, we were escorted into a small theater room along with some of the other guests. Shortly afterwards, the lower doors swung open, and in came the cast of *Just Mercy*. They walked by single file and began to shake hands with each and every person in the room. Then a handful of guests were selected to take pictures with the cast. I was fortunate enough to be one of them. We all stood in a large, loosely formed circle and began to have serious conversation about the film. I was truly honored to be in the room. After a while, we were led to a larger theater where the movie was going to be played. So we grabbed our popcorn and took our seats. We all engaged in light conversation as the movie was being prepared.

Moments later, Kobe entered the theater. After a few minutes, the entire cast went to the front of the theater, and Michael B. Jordan gave a few opening remarks. He then turned it over to Kobe Bryant. Kobe began to speak about his involvement with the event and why it meant so much to him. Once he was done speaking, it became apparent that he would not be staying for the duration of the film. As he was making his way out of the theater, he shook hands, thanking people for coming. I saw this as a good chance to meet him officially since he was not a part of the earlier meet and greet. But there were quite a few people in front of me, and they had begun holding longer conversations with Kobe than I expected. I decided to sit back down and save it for another day. I lived near L.A., and Kobe was becoming a fixture within film production industry. I turned to Levette and said, "I'll get him next time." Kobe chatted for a few more brief moments and then left the theater. That was Monday, January 6, 2020.

Three Weeks Later

Sunday, January 26, 2020.

I'll never forget this day. We were at church, and the services had just ended. When we left the sanctuary and spilled out into the foyer, everyone seemed to be looking at their phones. People looked shocked. As I started towards the door, someone asked me if I had heard the news. Then one of the members came up to me and said, "I can't believe this, man. Kobe Bryant died today."

I didn't believe it at first. Of course, being that many of them knew that I was just with him a few weeks back, I thought they were joking, and it was *not* funny at all. But I could tell be the way everyone else was reacting that this was real. I quickly pulled out my phone, and it was confirmed. Kobe had died in a helicopter crash that morning. That was a gut punch. Add to this the fact that his young daughter passed away with him as well, and it hurt even more. Of course, there were others on the helicopter, and I felt for their families too. But you can imagine why my focus was on Kobe and why his passing had such an impact. I was literally just with the guy. The eeriness of it all, for me personally, was overwhelming.

Driving home from church, all I could think about was Kobe. I felt like I knew the guy even though I had never officially met him. I think anyone who had watched Kobe play so often and for so long felt like they knew him in a certain way. Well I had been five feet away from getting to know him personally, and I forfeited that opportunity, assuming that there would for sure be a next time. Missing a chance to talk to Kobe is not what bothered me. What rattled me was the reality of knowing that I had said to myself, *I'll see him again,* only to find him gone three weeks later. And when I thought about Kobe's life, one that was spent playing basketball for the most part and building a future for his family, I'm saddened that he didn't get a chance to enjoy the next chapter, post-basketball. I'm sure he had plans for his little girls, his wife, and his business. But he could not have planned for that day.

You and I have a similar day coming. It's planned for us, but we can't plan for it. At least, from a human perspective. You never know when your number will be called. If Kobe had that information, he wouldn't have allowed anyone to get on the helicopter. Unfortunately, we can't prepare for our death day in that manner. In the same way, we can't know the date or time of the return of Christ either. Nobody knows when Christ will come back so that we can mark it on the calendar as our "get right" expiration date.

But spiritually, we can prepare for it all. That preparation for me consisted of accepting Jesus as the Lord of my life and never turning away from that faith, trust, and belief. It's striving to live a life that authenticates the faith that I claim to have. And it's doing all of this with the idea that at any moment, my days could be done. And should that ever be the case, I know that Jesus will be pleased with me and will say, "Well done." With every day of my life, I try to do what God has purposed for me to do in that moment. I try not to put off anything that God is leading me to do. That's what living with an eternal mindset is all about. It's never about depending on "getting it done the next time." Especially when it comes to being right with Jesus. Please, if you don't know Jesus or you know that you are not right with him, and you feel him trying to "meet" with you, don't say, *I'll get with him next time.* That time might never come.

FIX YOUR EYES

As the title of this book indicates, I wanted to encourage you to "lock in" and narrow your vision. Yes, you could even say be narrow minded. I can easily think of one instance of when being locked in, narrow focused, uncompromising, and unchanging is *good*. It is when referring to your allegiance, trust, faith, obedience, and commitment to following Jesus. For me, this is not the time to look for other options. There is none. Jesus is the way. That's it. From the beginning, Satan has been using, "But what about this" to tempt us into widening our focus, to get us looking at other options to accompany the God-approved options. We don't need other options. Looking for other options shows a clear lack of faith in God.

In my career, I have seen plenty of actors who claim to know Christ, yet much of what they openly do in life is completely contrary to Scripture. But if it appears to work for them, if they have what the world calls success, it becomes the hardest thing to convince a person to stop doing those things. Satan knows this and tends to help any willing compromiser succeed at doing it "their way." Since I was once like this in my early life, I know what it looks like. And it has been my experience over the years that one of the biggest reasons Satan is winning at knocking people off course is because he has too many ways to distract us. That's why I have narrowed my sight in the area of faith. I only put my faith in God, his Word, the Son, and the Holy Spirit. Everything else has no place if it distracts me from my faith.

I'm reminded of a horse race when I talk about fixing my eyes forward. Horses wear the "blinders" when they race to keep them focused on running their own individual race. I aim to live my life that way. I'm putting on the spiritual blinders. I don't even want to see Satan's options. I don't desire an easier path or an alternate route. But Satan doesn't care what you want or don't want. He aims temptation at us based on what *he* wants, which is for us to fall and fail in our walk with Christ. And there are many things all around us that he can use to accomplish his agenda. Minds that are open too wide are easy targets.

Call me what you want. Close-minded. Intolerant. When it comes to Satan and sin, I will agree with you. I don't want anything he has to offer. I'm trying not to look at anything influenced by him. I'm running my own race. And I aim to finish well. Lord's will, I can inspire a lot of people to run their races by the same standards. Hebrews 12:1–2 says, "Let us run with perseverance the race marked out for us, fixing our eyes on Jesus, the pioneer and perfecter of faith" (NIV). This has become one of my favorite Scripture verses and one of my many spiritual models for every area of my life.

Don't Let Satan Compromise *You*

If you know me well enough, you'll hear me use the word "uncompromised" quite a bit these days. This also happens to be the name of a program that I created in 2019, designed to help Christian actors and actresses who face the same types of challenges that I have. But what exactly does it mean to be uncompromised? It means not settling for anything less than God's will, his plans, and his purposes. It means staying focused on the plan God has for you with no intentions of trading it for anything else. It means not only being a Christian man or woman when you are out in front but also when nobody else is looking. Romans 2:16 is a Scripture verse that helps me remember this:

> This is the message I proclaim—that the day
> is coming when God, through Christ Jesus,
> will judge everyone's secret life. (NLT)

Uncompromised means loving and fearing God enough to say "no" to any opportunity that might cause you to sin and bring shame to Jesus' name. It means no dollar amount can ever buy away your obedience to the Bible. It means that no fear will keep you quiet when the Holy Spirit prompts you to speak up. It means that no level of human logic will ever replace the solid foundation of Scripture as the guiding principle of your life. It means that you will no longer conform to the patterns of this world, but instead, you will be changed by the renewing of your mind. It means that you would never trade God's way for an easier way. A different way. A shorter way. The more popular way. A more palatable way. A more accommodating way. A more acceptable way. A more understandable way.

All those options may make things seem easier, but that's the satanic trap. I don't want Satan's easy—I want God's *purpose*. If God's purpose is easy, then that's the icing. But regardless—I want whatever I do in life to be ordained by God. That's always the target I'm aiming for, and I refuse to let anything take my focus off that goal. *My eyes are fixed.*

What It All Amounts To

At this stage of my life, my career, my marriage, my parenting, my teaching, my relationships, my goals, dreams, desires, passions—my everything—falls under these three biblical principles: God is sovereign. Jesus is Lord. The Holy Spirit leads.

All my life, Satan has aimed to keep me from embracing these three things. And just because these things have become the pillars of my life, it doesn't stop Satan from trying to break them. But he can keep trying. I don't welcome the difficulty that his attacks bring my way, but I do welcome the testimonies that they create once Jesus gets involved. I know it is a cliché, but this saying is true: There is no testimony without a *test*. As you can see, I have certainly had my fair share.

I have been through a lot in my life. Plenty of ups; plenty of downs. Maybe you have too. Looking back on my own life always simultaneously amazes and inspires me. I'm amazed at how God was with me every step of the way, revealing (at his own pace and timing) the proper path that I needed to take in order to follow his plan for my life. I'm amazed at how he never let Satan fully knock me off course. Whenever I did make wrong turns, that spiritual GPS called the Holy Spirit would guide me back to the right road. And even when I did not know God the way I should have, he still loved me enough to give me the much-needed grace and mercy so that I could eventually realize what it truly meant to know him.

I am inspired by the fact that God has never failed to take care of me and my family. His guidance, strength, power, and purposes have become the pillars of my life. His goodness, kindness, faithfulness, patience, and undeserved love have given me every reason to give back to him everything I have. Everything I have been through in my life has led me to understand that there is only one way to do all of this.

With my eyes fixed.

Permanently fixed. Fixed on my heavenly Father, his purposes, his Word, his Spirit, and on living with an unwavering commitment to honoring him in every area of my life, while using every gift I have for the glory of his Son, Jesus Christ.

When I fail, I will repent. But I won't let Satan keep reminding me of my shortcomings. I'll look at the cross and remember that Jesus died so that I can have the power to turn away from any sin and shame. As a result, just as the Lord has always done, he will give me the strength, courage, guidance, and endurance necessary to continue this wonderful journey of purpose.

Chapter 13

UNSCRIPTED

Well.

This chapter is definitely about to live up to its titling. I have no plan for it.

I don't even know where to begin. Maybe I should start by telling you this book was only meant to be twelve chapters long. In fact, it was all but finished. But something happened that caused me to pull the manuscript back out and add a final chapter, which I am doing right now. Because on April 15, 2020, my mother died of complications caused by the COVID-19 virus. Three weeks later, my grandmother died too.

As many may know, it was the months of February and March of 2020 when the coronavirus began to take over our country. Quickly, it took over the world. Things began to shut down. Remember at first, it didn't seem to be that bad. The government didn't seem to be too concerned about it. But then people started to die. Everywhere. Then the quarantining began to increase worldwide. My state was one of the first hot spots. We were told to mask up and stay indoors. I remember staying glued to the news every day, all day. If I wasn't working on this book, I was watching the news. There was nothing else I could do. The entertainment industry had shut down. Everyone was trying to figure out how to survive. This started to feel like a disaster movie. People began running out to the stores and buying up everything. It was crazy. People were acting like the world was coming to an end.

I have family in Ohio, and my wife's mother lives in Kentucky. My wife and I constantly kept an eye on how things were back east. We saw that Ohio was having a higher rate of infections and deaths. I constantly called my mother to tell her everything I knew about the virus. My mother was seventy-three years old, and she had quite a few health complications. But everything wrong with my mother was internal, so it was very easy for her to hide her ailments.

Throughout the pandemic, it became clear that senior citizens with a high level of pre-existing conditions were among the most vulnerable to COVID-19. They were dying left and right. I became extremely concerned for my mother. I knew she had a few ailments, but I didn't know that she was hiding many more. Not from everyone did she hide the sicknesses, but mainly from me. That's just how she was with me. Rather than "worry me" (her words, not mine), she'd put on a happy face. But I knew her. I always knew when she was in pain or struggling. I just didn't know exactly what was causing it. And if I were to dig too deep, she would get frustrated and stressed, so I'd always back off. But when the virus started killing people within her age bracket and health status, I decided to take the risk of inquiring about her health once again without backing down this time should she not want to talk. I did, and it led to an extremely rare argument. She got angry, and we stopped talking for a day.

Meanwhile, I was watching the news, and more people her age were dying. The numbers of the infected and dead were going up, and the virus was becoming more mysterious and less containable. The term "asymptomatic" started to arise, meaning now there were people walking around who had the virus and didn't even know it or show any symptoms of it.

It had been a day since my mother and I had spoken or texted, and I couldn't help but wonder if she knew the latest updates. I called her and made sure that we quickly pushed aside the previous day's disagreement. I apologized for trying to force her to address her health, and she apologized for being a bit too stubborn. It was an easy transition because we had a great relationship. But what she did next floored me. She decided to share a good portion of her health issues with me. She texted me a page. Then another. Then another. Then another. I could not believe how many ailments she had and how many medications she was taking for each of the ailments. It pains me to even talk about this right now. I was about to list some of her ailments here, but I can't even type them. It's hard enough to even think about them.

My fear for her life went through the roof. All through-out the month of March, I talked or texted with her daily. Her husband (my stepfather) was pretty much in the same boat as she was. He had ailments that I had no clue about. At this stage of the virus, people were still working at essential businesses. My stepfather worked with such a place, delivering food to the elderly. When I found out from the latest reporting that the virus could easily be brought in and out of homes unknowingly, I wanted him to stop working. I also wanted my mother to stop leaving the house. My hope was that she had people around her who could run all her errands. From a financial perspective, I hoped that we could have a talk about how much money they would need so my stepfather could stop working.

Neither of them was willing to have this conversation. It didn't seem that deep to them. As I pushed and pressed, I could feel tension building. I could tell from the tone of the conversation that if my mother wanted to go to the store, she was going to do it. And according to my mother, my stepfather's pride would not allow me to dig too deeply into a financial conversation with him. He wanted to work and provide for his own household, which is commendable. But now wasn't the time for that kind of thinking. They both needed to be at home.

Convincing them of this was not easy either because they could turn on the news at the time and see divergent, non-united opinions about the severity of the virus. They kept hearing about how it was going to go away soon. So my stepfather kept working, and my mother would occasionally take quick trips to the grocery store. I couldn't stop them, so I at least bugged them about masking and disinfecting. I told my mother that she needed to make sure that whenever my stepfather came home from work, they would immediately throw whatever clothes he was wearing into the washer. She never confirmed if the two of them were doing that. Instead of answering directly, she would pivot. She told me not to worry so much about her. She was fine. She just wanted to continue to hear about me and how my family was getting along. It was hard to talk to her like this. I was laughing with her and trying to talk with her as usual, but in the back of my mind, I literally was worried about her dying.

My mother knew how I felt. I told her that I did not want this thing to kill her or anyone in her house. My ninety-three-year-old grandmother (with Alzheimer's and a few other ailments herself) lived there too. I warned my mother that the virus could potentially take out her whole household. But, as you would agree, I couldn't keep talking to her about death all the time. Nobody would want that. So I continued to check on her and cloaked my concerns within the framework of a simple question: "Y'all safe?"

Now all I could do was respect her answer. I just tried to leave the door open in case she needed help. I reminded her that if she needed anything to let me know. Prayer was all I had. I just never felt confident that my family was taking this virus seriously enough. I never wanted to get a call from her telling me that she had caught this virus. But soon, that would be the exact call that I would get. The last words that I ever heard my mother say was, "Y'all need to start praying because I got the virus."

I assured her that I would pray without ceasing. We said our "love yous" and goodbyes, and she began her treatment. I was so angry after hanging up the phone. I had known that all of this could happen, and now it had. But before I could finish getting mad about that, I learned that my stepfather had the virus as well. Now both of them were hospitalized, and because of the unorthodox hospital situation, they were admitted to separate hospitals.

I was devastated. I prayed for calm, but I was so angry that it had come to this. Planes were grounded, so I couldn't even go see my mother. Come to find out that it would not have mattered anyway because no visitors were allowed on the COVID treatment floors. The news wasn't helping. The more I watched, the more afraid for their lives I became. Nothing seemed organized, and no one seemed to know anything. I was hearing that all kinds of different treatments were being used because the virus was new and scientists were still discovering many things concerning it.

Then the scariest part of it all happened. My mother began to develop life-threatening complications, and doctors put her into a medically induced coma. This hurt my heart so bad because every person who had reached this stage had died.

I can't write about this part anymore. Let's just cut to the chase. She spent her birthday in the hospital (April 9), and she passed away six days later, on April 15. My grandmother died a few weeks later on May 9. I was going to talk about my feelings about it, the fact that I couldn't see her, what happened with the funeral, and a bunch of other stuff, but I'm sorry. I can't. It is too painful.

I had a feeling this might happen, that's why I entitled this chapter "Unscripted." I didn't plan to lose her. I didn't plan to write about her in this way. That's why throughout this book (up until this point), I talk about her as if she were alive. Because she was. Her passing on, from this life to the next, absolutely needed to be included—no matter how sloppy my attempt to talk about it may be. My life story doesn't exist without her part. From start to finish. *That woman loved me.*

The best way for me to wrap this up is to share with you a poem that I wrote. I don't know how else to end this chapter. I hope sharing this with you will suffice:

(Written by T.C. Stallings in memory of his mother. Mother's Day, 2020.)

A year removed from just having your fourth baby,
adopted a fifth, conceived number six;
But my life became "a maybe," representing a risk.
Fear drove you crazy, economic life hazy;
Doubts rollin' in on the daily,
stemming from questions about raising me.
You felt your life was not ready, and Dad's life was not right;
What if I didn't turn out right?
Abortion thoughts you had to fight.
Maybe a preemie baby at best,
with something wrong with my chest,
Or something wrong with my brain;
you didn't want that potential pain;
But you fought to find the courage,
and through Christ you saw the light,
Told yourself God just might have a purpose for my life;
You let him finish the good work he started in you
and never looked back;
In fact, you changed your life
so that my world could be intact.
You did all that.

Cheerleader. My biggest. Always the loudest in the crowd;
You believed, so I achieved, anything to make you proud;
Did all I could to make you smile,
make you sing, or do that thing
you always did when I succeeded,
big banners so I could read it;
Touchdown, T.C.! Hand the ball to the ref;
Next thing I would always hear: "Gone 'head wit cho self!"
Now you're gone wit cho self. Only I hated to see you go.
I'd be all messed up if not for a few facts that I know.
Before me, you knew God,
accepted his Spirit, and met Jesus.
Because of that, you're in a better place;
can't help but let that please us!
You got no struggles, no tears, no problems, no fears,
No sickness, no pain, no worries on the brain;
Your body fell to the grave,
but your soul had a better landing,
Making the hurt from your departure bow
to a peace beyond understanding!
No doubt, your death floored me,
but I know you went home to glory;
Just because it's a novel virus
don't mean it gets to write your story!
You are more than just another victim of a horrific pandemic;
You're a heaven-bound soldier
who just landed smack dab in it!
My mother. A lover. A hugger. A giver.
A friend;

Sometimes stubborn, but knew when to say when;
I miss the little things you did,
the way you laugh, the way you sing;
That simple little text you always left that said,
"I really didn't want anything."
That big ol' smiling face, two dimples in every grin;
But my heart holds on to the promise of God,
That through Christ, I'll see you again.
Rest in Christ, Mama.

In the most loving memory possible of my mother,
Sylvia Ann Thompson.

STORY GALLERY

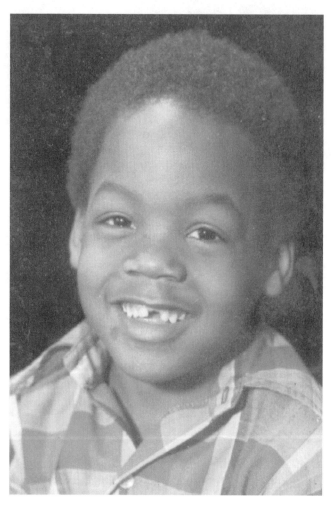

This is the little barefoot wanderer. And yes, I loved my free sandwiches.

Sunday morning, practicing my ushering duties before church.

Where it all started! That's me, #2, a member of the
Warrensville Bobcats city football team.

My wife, the hooper. When I told you that Levette meant business on the court—I was *NOT* playing.

Levette and I have been through so much together.
It's fitting that our favorite activities include roller coasters.

My huge python helped electrify my entrance as the team celebrated my nationally televised win on Animal Planet's *King of the Jungle*.

The most enjoyable jobs (aside from football) were always the ones involving either animals or kids. (NOT BANANAS!)

My wife's dad, "Big Joe," made sure that I knew the importance of taking real good care of his daughter.

Here I am with my "Insight Cable" uniform on.
Hated selling cable, but I love the little girl I'm building a snowman with.

After previously being blessed with a baby girl, finding out that I was going
to have a baby boy next brought me so much joy!

Competing and landing a few awards at the AMTC in Florida.
This acting competition was my first big step towards becoming an actor.

Pictured here with an MVP trophy from a five-touchdown performance. The day *before* this game, my wife told me I was having a boy!

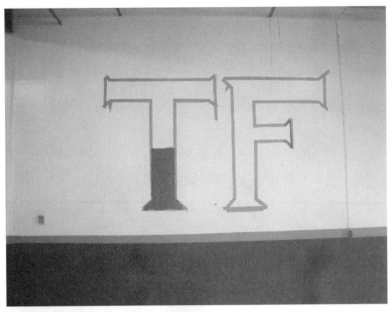

Levette and I put in so much work transforming a dusty, run-down warehouse into a viable place to start our own business, Triumph Fitness.

The transformation turned out so *beautiful*. God's handprint was undeniably everywhere. It was hard to leave this and move to Hollywood.

I'll never forget the day we officially opened Triumph Fitness and officially became business owners! Indescribable joy for my whole family.

Levette and I enjoyed our first ever red carpet movie premiere for
Courageous. We had no idea it would be the first of many!

In February of 2003, I entered the ministry. During the tough times, my most peaceful moments occurred when teaching about Jesus.

The accident that changed my perspective forever.
My acting career would begin a week later.

Transforming into T.J. for the movie *Courageous* was quite the process. I'll never forget my first big role!

Winning Animal Planet's *King of the Jungle* took me to places
that I had never been, such as New Zealand and Australia.

This is the game that I should *not* have been playing in.
Cost me two broken ribs and the worst pain *ever*.

The success of *War Room* was massive, leading to me addressing large crowds in Time Square, NYC, and countless TV interviews.

My summers in Louisville, KY, were often spent working or volunteering at the Louisville Zoo. (I trained goats to do "high fives.")

I'm so grateful that my mother loved church *so much*.
Her example taught me how to love it too.

My time with her ended much like it started. In her arms.
The picture on the right is the last time I would see my mother. *(For now.)*

ABOUT THE AUTHOR

T.C. Stallings is a former professional athlete now finding success in film and television. T.C. made his feature film debut in the 2011 hit movie *Courageous*, portraying the memorable character T.J. But T.C.'s career reached new heights with his breakout performance as Tony Jordan in the 2015 hit film *War Room*, which soared to #1 at the box office. Following this feat, T.C. released his first book, *The Pursuit*. His second quickly followed, entitled *Playing on God's Team*. He also began pursuing the ambitious goal of opening doors for other actors and actresses by creating the groundbreaking actor coaching program called Uncompromised: Christian Actor Coaching. In 2019, his production company (Team TC

Productions & Purpose Studios) reached a milestone when he wrote, directed, and self-produced a documentary called *24 Counter: The Story Behind the Run*, which received a film festival nomination for Most Inspirational Documentary. In 2020, T.C. became an Executive Producer and Show Runner for the newly formed PAX-TV Network. T.C. is also a nation-wide brand ambassador for Clearplay, a company with the mission of providing families with clean, wholesome entertainment options. T.C. is a wide-ranging actor and huge advocate for clean family entertainment, and he enjoys getting creatively involved in philanthropic efforts around the world.

OTHER BOOKS
BY T.C. STALLINGS

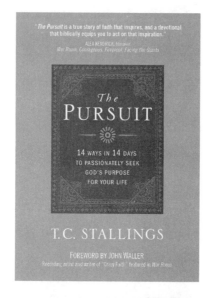